GORDON
BUSINESS AS USUAL

RUTH CHIPPERFIELD

Ballpoint Press

Published in 2014 by Ballpoint Press
4 Wyndham Park, Bray, Co Wicklow, Republic of Ireland.
Telephone: 00353 86 821 7631
Email: ballpointpress1@gmail.com
Web: www.ballpointpress.ie

ISBN 978-0-9926732-7-7

Book design and production by Elly Design

Cover photograph: Gordon, photographed by Salome Stephens Murphy, Social Care Manager, Peacehaven Trust Ltd

Printed and bound by GraphyCems

peacehaventrust
WWW.PEACEHAVENTRUST.COM

CONTENTS

INTRODUCTION

FOR more than thirty years Gordon travelled by public transport around Dublin, and into County Wicklow, always busy, always planning the next trip. He was well-known and completely at home on the trains and buses. The staff were his friends. This small man, now aged sixty-one, has an intellectual disability. He believed himself to be a businessman like his dad. So he was seen striding through the streets dressed in a suit, carrying a briefcase, a rolled umbrella and the day's copy of The Irish Times.

Gordon has had adventures that his family couldn't have dreamed of. He's had sorrows, and joyful times and occasions of high comedy. I've been beside him for much of the time, because Gordon is my very special brother.

Ruth Chipperfield

October 2014

TESTIMONIALS

ST MICHAEL'S HOUSE

RUTH Chipperfield's biography of her brother Gordon's life is an uplifting account of family life with a child with Special Needs in 1950's Ireland. It's a memoir of a life of caring – from devoted neighbours to adoring friends – of faith, strength, love, acceptance, stability and good sense.

Gordon is a unique, independent and affectionate character who is loved by his family. As he travels each day on his business adventures, he makes friends and is loved wherever he goes. He is an unforgettable person. For his family, it's a road of struggle, humour and the unknown, but with their careful guiding hands, Gordon's independence and spirit is nurtured.

This book is a reminder of the goodwill and enormous struggle that so many families have and how with unconditional care and acceptance, each individual like Gordon can go to the beat of their own drum, make their own choices, enjoy their life, and reach their full potential.

Having worked in this field for over thirty-eight years, this book reminds me how privileged I have been to work among people like Gordon and how fortunate I have been in seeing their unique gifts.

Patricia Doherty,
Chief Executive Officer, St. Michael's House

BUS ÁTHA CLIATH

I READ Gordon's Story on holiday in Wales and somehow the spirit of the book matched perfectly the surroundings and the glorious weather. Gordon's Story is full of optimism, determination, faith and music and also describes with great humour how Gordon, after a difficult birth, went on to have a very positive life. This story will be a great inspiration to many people who face similar challenges.

The contribution of the bus timetables to his developing understanding of geography, numbers, and moving around is brilliant and a use nobody in this organisation could possibly have imagined!

Gordon is remembered fondly by many people in Donnybrook Garage particularly for marshalling queues and ensuring that courtesy reigns wherever he goes.

Music is a constant throughout the book so Gordon will never be an 'unsung' hero after this fine biography is released!

Paddy Doherty
Chief Executive, Bus Átha Cliath

IARNRÓD ÉIREANN

*"If Gordon's life was a tapestry,
the pattern would be stitched by trains."*

WHILST reading this charming book, I was struck by this quote. Train travel was central to every fibre of Gordon's being and contributed much joy to the tapestry of life.

The railway is a lot more than trains, track, signals and platforms. It is about people. The people who work every day to keep the trains moving, and our customers who are central to everything we do. Gordon's lifelong love for trains started very early in his life and it was something that grew with him throughout his life. His trip by train every day into the city centre was so much part of his routine, but his adventures did not stop there, he undertook journeys all over the network, making lots of friends along the way.

It is enchanting to read the anecdotes of his friendship with the staff members at Greystones and how he became part of the railway family, how drivers would toot their horn when they saw Gordon on the platform and how staff members, particularly in the city centre stations were so concerned and mindful for Gordon.

I have never had the pleasure of meeting Gordon, but from speaking to colleagues, he was a familiar and welcome figure that is well known all across the network. His tale reminds us all that no matter what obstacles are placed in our way in life, the friendship and support of family and community strengthens all of us, and allows us to enrich each other's lives.

The railway community in Iarnród Éireann are proud to have been a part of Gordon's life, and are privileged that he has chosen to be part of ours.

David Franks
Chief Executive, Iarnród Éireann

ACKNOWLEDGEMENTS AND THANKS

I ESPECIALLY want to thank Louis Hemmings, poet and bookman, for his steady encouragement. I remember him at an early stage reading through the script and saying in disgust 'No! No! No!' He quickly put manners on my writing. Then he stepped back, and off I went with confidence, enjoying every minute. I trusted Louis's judgement, and sometimes I followed his advice. Louis, thank you.

My husband Keith was angelically patient. He lost me for hours day after day. And he lost the use of the computer for those hours. He read the manuscript, and exposed errors and inconsistencies. He made it a better book. He has a marvellous memory, and helped me out with details that I had forgotten. Gordon's much-loved brother-in-law.

My family were delighted at what I was doing, and they encouraged me. They all love books. I hope they weren't too worried that I would disgrace us all.

My daughter Abigail Chipperfield Smith created the page simulating Gordon's desk. On it are all the things central to his life, in exquisite detail. I have to thank her for the book's title.

After submitting my manuscript to various publishers, I sent it to Ballpoint Press. PJ Cunningham replied, and I was astonished to read, 'By coincidence I knew Gordon, as I used the DART and the Wexford train. You are right, the railway staff treated him as one of their own... I think we should sit down and talk about the next step.' We met and talked, met and talked. PJ saw me as an Author. It's been a delight to work with him, and I am immensely proud to be published by Ballpoint Press.

The book you are holding is the work of the graphic designer Joe Coyle. He has realised dreams I didn't know I had. The unique briefcases are Joe's creation, and they are pure joy.

Every person, whose actions and speech are recounted in the book, has given me permission to make use of them. I am truly grateful.

Dr Stuart Neilson, Computer Scientist and Mathematician, graciously allowed me to connect his love of Mathematics with Gordon's obsession with numbers.

The elegant appearance of Will Cochran's Whistling Tune on page 20 is thanks to Jacqueline Mullen, musician. She turned my handwritten scribbles into print. I appreciate this, as until now the melody had only existed in my head.

Gordon made innumerable journeys by Irish Rail and Dublin Bus, and many of the staff were his trusted friends. I want to thank them here for their immense kindness to him. These wonderful friends were Gordon's daily companions. They made his life rich, they gave meaning to his days, they welcomed him into their workplaces, they recognised him as one of themselves. It was a unique brotherhood, where the employees of two separate companies individually and collectively embraced one small man.

Bewley's in Grafton Street was a happy place for Gordon, so I thank Bewley's for the kindness of its staff, especially the inimitable Ms Tattins Twomey.

I'm grateful to Mr Patrick Bewley for permission to include Tattins's photo, which features in 'The Legendary Lofty Clattery Café', by Tony Farmar.

The Irish Times was Gordon's newspaper of choice. He never missed buying it, and when he became ill and stopped going to the shops, the paper of record was delivered to his home in Greystones every day. The Irish Times staff couldn't have known that Gordon was addicted to their publication, but I do thank them and acknowledge the place it has had in his life. When she was teaching Gordon to 'read', the textbook his mother used was The Irish Times.

God be in my head, and in my understanding;
God be in my eyes, and in my looking;
God be in my mouth, and in my speaking;
God be in my heart, and in my thinking;
God be at mine end, and at my departing.

Sarum primer, 1558

PROLOGUE

Let's hear the Hallelujah Chorus!

The upstairs window is wide open and music is pouring out. I can see a man inside, close to the window. He's wearing thick glasses and in one hand he's holding a big floppy book. With the other he's vigorously conducting a choir and orchestra. He's singing his heart out.

* * *

'Daddy, Daddy, Michael's coming!' I was jumping with excitement.

It was September 1953 and our mother was pregnant. My sister and I had waited so long for the baby to arrive. We were sure it would be a boy, and for some reason it seemed natural to call him Michael. We didn't know his gender, of course, you didn't in those days.

So in late September, 1953, when I was twelve, we were awakened in the dark night by the news that the baby was going to be born. *Michael was coming!*

He was a boy. This is his story.

Bundy the dog

Mummymummy

44A Clery's

BANK EBS

Hallelujah Chorus!

Bewley's Special Olympics

BRIEFCASES

AHO

28 Blackheath Gardens

David, pianist with crossed hands

The Irish Times

1

A FARMHOUSE IN COUNTY WICKLOW

'NO thank you, I don't want a big hat!'

'But Lydia, it would look lovely. A wide brim, navy, with your beautiful blue frock.'

'No, mammy, I really can't. Not a big one. Will would hate it, and I wouldn't feel like me. People would laugh, it would blow off – it's *my wedding!*'

As if that had anything to do with it. Lydia may have been the bride, and her bridegroom, Will, may have had strong views on hats, but ... on the day Lydia looked very beautiful, in a long misty blue crepe frock, carrying a pink and blue bouquet, and wearing a navy blue hat with a wide dipping brim. It was perfect.

My parents, Will and Lydia, were married in St Mary's Church of Ireland in Blessington, County Wicklow in September 1937. The village was in the depths of the country; today it's practically a suburb of Dublin. This was where Lydia was born to Henry and Elizabeth Egar, the fourth of six children. Over time a wide area which included a small village and much of Henry's farmland was slowly submerged by the creation of a reservoir. This was done by damming the River Liffey waterfall at Poulaphouca, the Puck's Hole. The resulting lake served the hydroelectric plant for the Electricity Supply Board and also as a major source for Dublin's water supply, and parts of it were developed as a water-sports facility. This was a time of great change for many families.

Fortunately Lydia's father wasn't solely involved in farming; for years he was a postman.

In times of severe drought when the water-level went down, the skeletons of houses poked up from their spectacular grave. This dam work started in the first year of my parents' marriage and took ten years to complete. While Lydia was learning to be married, the childhood places she had known were being slowly drowned.

Lydia was twenty-four and Will was thirty-one at the time of their marriage. Four years later I, Ruth Elizabeth, was born on the first of September.

Life was good. My parents' close friends became my honorary aunts and uncles. Our home was in Killester, in North Dublin, in Furry Park. What a lovely address for a baby to have! All the houses should have been thatched, and in the gardens there would be teddy bears instead of gnomes. The house was happy and welcoming. Friends and family came often, and they knew that along with the welcome would be Lydia's irresistible home-made scones.

Scones became a leitmotif of this marriage. In joy and in sorrow, Lydia responded by baking scones. The busier she was, and the more she wanted to comfort people, the more delicious they were. Warm and buttery, their fragrance said to people who appeared on the doorstep 'Come on in, you're welcome, it's lovely to see you!'

Seasoned bakers will endorse the theory that, when it's made in a hurry and with a light touch, a perfect scone results. Will was known to carry a scone in his pocket, to deal with sudden hunger pangs. The scones were most often baked and buttered to feed the group of young men and women who gathered in my parents' home. They chatted and played games and listened to music and shared their thoughts, and Will led them in studying the Bible, and they talked together about following Jesus.

As a group they went on Outings. Hardly anybody had a car, so they all went by bike, as far as their energy would take them. They didn't go to pubs or hotels for lunch, they brought picnics. Some black and white photos survive showing them sprawled comfortably on some grassy bank, overlooking the sea in Howth, or in the depths of Wicklow, the Garden of Ireland.

Will and Lydia bought a piano for £50 with some wedding present money; the generous aunt being thereafter known as the Fifty-Pound Auntie. Will loved to share music with their young friends. He trained a choir, amateur in the true sense of the word, and introduced the singers to oratorios. They sang Stainer's *Crucifixion,* and *Olivet to Calvary* by J.H. Maunder. My dad had no formal musical training. He was in his early thirties by this time. His reading about music and listening to it and studying to perform it had enriched his understanding and skills, so he was well-equipped to present these works. They were beautiful, and not particularly difficult. Making music glued these people together, and they became friends for life.

The performances took place in Fairview Hall, which was Will and Lydia's church, a red brick building looking like a Victorian Mission Hall. It wasn't called a church, because the people who worshipped there saw themselves as belonging to the worldwide Christian church. So it was called a Hall. People went to meetings, not services, and they sang their hearts out, hymns by Charles Wesley, Fanny Crosby and Isaac Watts. And they also sang quantities of hymns set to melodies which were musically undistinguished, but strongly rhythmic and easy to sing, by such as those by Ira D. Sankey and P.P. Bliss.

Men taught from the Bible. They didn't preach, they *spoke*, as in 'Who's speaking on Sunday?' Preaching was for people who attended churches with steeples. There was no liturgy, and there were no rules, but there were habitual ways of doing things. Groups of people who meet together regularly generally form habits and then if they're not careful they invent rules, then they feel they have to enforce the rules. The members of this congregation were happy and comfortable with the habits. There wasn't any Ruling Body, they read the Bible for themselves, and there was lovingkindness and trust between them.

I was a big strong infant, and my mother breast-fed me for a few months, until a breast abscess ended that particular pleasure. She cried while she and my dad coaxed me into accepting a bottle.

I became attractively plump, which was considered to be desirable for babies, and Lydia became a little bit plump too. Sitting up in my big boat-like pram I waited at the gate of our house every evening to welcome my dada home. He announced his arrival by whistling his signature tune. His mother, Lizzie, had composed it, and had probably made a poem to go with it. It was a circular melody, which meant that the end led back into the beginning, so it could be whistled over and over again, depending on how fast my father walked.

Exile

About a year after I was born, Will was transferred to the Belfast branch of the Caledonian Insurance Company, for which he worked. He went ahead of my mother and me, to find a house and to sort out the details of the move. This was in 1942 and the Second World War was raging. In the previous year, at Easter, a raid by German bombers had left parts of Belfast in a sea of flames. The second of two raids caused death and destruction comparable to that suffered by some of the large British cities. Little streets of red-brick homes were wrecked; part of the Antrim Road was wiped out, and the roof of the City Hall became a dreadful beacon of flames.

Houses to rent were scarce. In fact, it seems to have been the worst possible time to move a family to live in Belfast. I suspect that my parents' decision to rent a house rather than buying showed that they had no intention of spending the rest of their lives in exile. When Will found a spacious house to rent, in a pleasant suburb, it was undoubtedly a miracle. This new home was near the Antrim Road, which, I have no doubt, still showed the evidence of the previous year's grievous destruction.

After a while one of our new neighbours asked Will how he had managed to pull off such a coup – it was widely understood that there were no houses to be found! There hadn't been any secret pulling of strings. It was simply the answer to many anxious prayers. My mum and I went up on the train to join him. I toddled joyfully along the platform to fall into his arms, and at 13 Taunton Avenue our new life began.

It was far from restful for my parents. I slept badly, and Will would walk the floor with me in his arms, singing in the dead of the night the verses of John Keble's hymn,

'Sun of my soul, thou Saviour dear,
It is not night if Thou be near.
Oh may no earth-born cloud arise,
To hide Thee from Thy servant's eyes.

When the soft dews of kindly sleep
My wearied eyelids gently steep,
Be my last thought, how sweet to rest
For ever on my Saviour's breast.

Watch by the sick; enrich the poor
With blessings from Thy bounteous store;
Be every mourner's sleep tonight
Like infant slumbers, pure and light.'

The melody, Abends, by Herbert Oakeley, went straight to my heart. Will's voice was beautiful. When he stopped, naturally I began to cry again. He walked and walked and sang till I slept. He was so patient.

Then I found my thumb.

If you have never sucked a thumb, you've missed one of the great pleasures of life. To snuggle into a warm bed, and tuck in the perfectly shaped and sized thumb, and drift off to sleep was bliss. It wasn't my fault if the soggy digit fell out and I had to yell for my dad.

One of the bugbears of my childhood was bed-wetting. I went on doing it for so long, through birthday after birthday. My dad would come in response to my call, plug in the electric fire, get me out of bed, change my nightie, and organise a dry bed. That involved holding the heavy brick-red waterproof sheet in front of the red elements of the fire to dry it, while I shivered behind him. The hollow 'middle-of-the-dark-night' feeling, the radiant fire in the chilly room, and the distinctive mixture of smells, are vivid memories today. Will never showed any exasperation.

I bit my nails. Anything else? Oh, the occasional tantrum.

Was it from dealing with my antics that Will and Lydia learned lessons of patience? I'm surprised they didn't want to drown me. I was a pretty little thing, but not placid.

'Lydia darling, *I'm so sorry for you!*' said my aunt at my birthday party, when I was turning four. She had no children. She was the most gracious kind aunt a girl could have. Her outburst of sympathy for my mother wasn't because I was deathly ill. Something had vexed me, and I, the birthday girl, was sitting on the bottom step of the stairs, howling with temper and unmanageable, frightening grief.

Actually, there was something about the bottom step that suited me. When I was being good, my mother sometimes asked me to help with setting the tea- table, and I was given the butter-dish to carry into the dining room. As I passed through the hall, I strayed towards the stairs. Bottom step to sit on, butter-dish with its dear little blunt knife – an irresistible combination. How delicious it was. I've never really got over my love of butter.

A domestic chore I was trusted with was to fetch a couple of preserved eggs out of the crock in the under-stairs cupboard. The eggs were submerged in sodium silicate, which we knew as waterglass. Lydia dissolved the powder in water in the crock, and it turned into a jelly, and the fresh eggs were preserved, for weeks, maybe months, till we needed them. So on request I fished a couple out, and rinsed them under the tap for my mum to use. In this job I was completely trustworthy. I wasn't tempted by slithery raw eggs. They were for a Madeira-type cake, and my mum would beat and beat the mixture with a big spoon.

Wartime austerity with its food rationing meant in practical terms that we did without many delights. There are vivid stories of children swarming to sweetshops when the rationing of sugary things was lifted. My grandfather, Cuckoo, who lived with us, wasn't very excited about Jelly Babies or Spangles or Toffee Apples, but he longed for a banana. Not only for himself; he wanted to give me a banana. The day came when imported fruits trickled into Northern Ireland, and my Cuckoo got one banana.

I can see him smiling lovingly, delighted with himself, and so happy for me. He peeled the skin back and gave it to me. With all this build-up, you will have guessed it's not a happy story. It was disgusting. Nowadays, I have a civilised attitude towards the weird-tasting things, perfect convenience foods, and clearly there are some people who like them. Good mushy baby spoon-food (poor babies!) After that, there's nothing good to say. *Banana ice cream! Smoothies*, with sneaky banana in them! Yuck.

That brings me to another odd thing about our family life. For my mother, beating cakes was extra hard. Her right side shook when she was tense or troubled. It was a sort of pronounced tremble. I was familiar with this and couldn't imagine a mother who didn't quiver; I assumed that they all did. Mothers whose arms didn't quake were clearly extra tough. I was quite proud of my mother's emotional and sensitive nature.

I never discovered what caused the disability. Lydia had no name for it. She told me that when she was a young child she spent long periods of time in the Adelaide Hospital in Peter Street, in Dublin, being operated on, having 'lumps' on her right arm excised. There were concave white shiny scars dotted over the arm, which I was familiar with – that was just a normal mummy's arm. As for a diagnosis, would cystic tuberculosis come anywhere near an answer? Whatever the cause, the right side was weak and wobbly and difficult to control.

Many weeks in hospital, involving operations, with pain, and separation from her family must have had some impact on the little girl. Family couldn't visit often, Blessington seeming very far away in those days. There were other children to care for, and there were the outdoor work of the farm and her father's postal deliveries to get through. What passed through Lydia's four- or five-year-old head? Thinking about this recently, I've wondered if the 'shakes' of the damaged arm could have been psychosomatic, a child's reaction to fear and anxiety?

'Lydia, the doctor just wants to look at your arm.'

'No, don't let him touch me! *Go away!*'

'Now, Lydia, be a good girl...' The shakes, together with the weakness in the arm, were a very real disability, so in school the teacher insisted that she wrote with her left hand, not the wobbly right one. But Lydia was naturally right-handed.

That was an example of the offensive practice in the past of forcing left-handed children to use their right hands, 'right' for some obscure reason in this context meaning 'correct'. In her case, Lydia was a mirror-image of this. It was as destructive for her as for all the children over time who have been mentally and physically abused by this determined stupidity of grown-ups.

Every single morning while the little girl was in hospital, an uncle who had business in town came, by special permission, to the door of her ward, looked in and caught her watching eye, and with a big smile waved to her.

Friends and School

In Belfast, in Taunton Avenue, my parents made friends with our neighbours. My mother couldn't help making friends. I acquired honorary aunts and uncles, and an honorary Grannie, who had lived in Africa and had family there. How exotic! This grandmother's granddaughter, whose home was in Africa, is my friend today.

Our house was attached to the home of a brother and sister, Brian and Joan, and their parents. Brian and I hit it off delightfully, once I grew up a bit. We used to post notes to each other in the back garden hedge. Why we had to do that when we were living more or less contiguously, I don't know. Probably we would have found sending notes exciting even if we lived in the same house. He was older than I, and very clever, by comparison anyway.

Ann, my tall friend from across the road, was a true chum; she would walk in the gutter while I walked on the 'bias binding' of the footpath, so that our heads were close enough for us to chatter. Another girl, who was able to take her coat off while riding her bike, 'Look, No Hands!' was privileged: her dolls had an enormous bed to sleep in! After her stern father slapped her face one day, I decided there was little to envy. I liked to visit another house where a friend lived, also across the road. It had a wonderful sort of barn behind it, with an upstairs, and a half-door. At the end of the road, near the bend, lived another girl. Along with her unusually beautiful name, she had blonde curls. I had brown plaits. They did have curly ends.

Life in Belfast was complicated then by more than World War 2. The war was happening to us, from the outside. But on the inside, in people's hearts and minds, there were divisions and tensions, which we children didn't understand, but of which we were aware. I remember a group of children, which included me, singing rude songs about a boy whom we considered to be 'different'. Was it because his family was of a different religion to ours? We were horrible. It was done in ignorance, but we meant to be cruel.

The church which we joined, Victoria Memorial Hall, known as a Brethren Assembly, anchored us in this quite strange city. I attended Sunday school, and the names of other girls are in my head still. Years later some of these girls came from Belfast to an Easter Camp in Greystones, Co Wicklow. I was there, with my friends. We were aged about eleven. In the course of some rough and tumble one of the Belfast girls managed to damage her skirt. We were shocked – skirts didn't grow on trees. But she, with an insouciant toss of her head said 'Oh, don't worry. I'll get a new one!' I had never met such sophistication.

When my best friend Ann and I were aged about five, we started school. Ann went to a local primary school, Skegoniel, and I trotted up the road and round the corner to Holyrood school. Mrs Bowyer was the Head of this centre of enthusiastic progressive teaching. There were about 100 boys and girls, from five to 18. Some of the senior girls were awe-inspiring, seeming to be more grown-up and poised than even our parents were. I was intrigued that one of them sucked her thumb – like me! Their academic heights could only be imagined. I was happy there, and I blossomed, though that's belied by a school photo in which my front-row grumpy face looks like a bulldog. I was considered to be rather clever. Top of the form, of six children! Probably that made me a bit too charmed with myself.

Holyrood, being progressive, never taught me to write properly, which is why as I grew up I kept re-inventing my handwriting style, with no great distinction. I'm still working on it.

Years later it dawned on me that, thanks to all my little Taunton Avenue chums, I – an exile from that place known as 'The Sythe' – most surely spoke with a Belfast accent! Not only had I that mixture of sharpness and singsong cadences, but my ice cream between two wafers was a slider, and when it was in a cone it was a poke. My gym shoes were gutties. When we were hungry, we went to the kitchen door, like tradesmen, and asked for a piece, which was bread and jam.

For piano lessons I went up the road to Miss Ross. She was very old, graceful and grey-haired. I did pretty well at piano, because I could practice during the lunchtime break from school. I learned to love music, beginning with the cradle song sung to me by my father in the long ago nights. For years, after I went to bed, my lullabies would be Will playing the piano downstairs, going through the masters, Beethoven, Bach, Brahms, often Schubert ('heavenly café music'). Sometimes before bed I stood beside the piano to listen, and when he played a certain Beethoven Minuet in G, for some unaccountable reason I always wept.

My dad made me weep again, unforgettably. When I was in my teens he took me to a performance of Brahms's German Requiem, sung in English. The murmuring orchestra, joined by the opening swelling chorus, 'Blessed are they that mourn, for they shall be comforted', it broke my heart. And then mended it.

There was a succession of my parents' friends and relations from Dublin, who visited. Some stayed with us. My mother kept going, as she fed the guests and changed bed linen yet again, by taking Aspirin for chronic headaches.

Our friend Olive Nelson lived with us for a time. For me she was an extra parent. Later she became an honorary aunt, and eventually a big sister. In the morning, hours before getting-up time I would slither into Olive's bed and cajole and hector her to tell me stories. Sometimes she recited,

'There was an old woman who swallowed a fly,
I don't know why she swallowed a fly,
Perhaps she'll die.

'There was an old woman who swallowed a spider
That wriggled and jiggled and tickled inside her.
She swallowed the spider to catch the fly,
I don't know why she swallowed the fly,
Perhaps she'll die.'

She swallowed six more animals, each bigger than the last, until

'She swallowed a horse,
She's dead – of course!'

Lyrics by Rose Bonne

Olive sang to me as well, and the songs were a bit odd, they had no tune. In fact she simply hadn't a note, she cared nothing for music. The noise annoyed her. A big challenge for her was – to go to Heaven would be glorious, but how could she cope with the endless music, as in *harps*?

We were touched by death. My 'Cuckoo' grandfather, Samuel Cochran, who was living with us, had white hair, and a rich white moustache. He was very very old, over eighty. Because of, or in spite of the banana incident, I was slightly scared of him. Also, one day in the garden when I was carelessly swinging a heavy stick, to my – and his – horror, I struck his bad leg.

When he was near to death, he seemed to be very sad. As he wept, Lydia said 'But darling, you are going to meet the Lord!' The old man replied that he didn't want to leave his 'little cuckoo' – that was me, we were both cuckoos. After he died, I was able to bring my friends proudly upstairs to see his body, beautifully laid in the coffin. We climbed up on the stand to look at him; he was sheltered in silky white folds, wearing posh pyjamas. None of us fell in.

My Little Sister

Lydia had been told after my birth, in September 1941, that she shouldn't, or maybe couldn't, have any more children. I have no idea what the problem was; it never occurred to me to ask questions about it. She may not have known. Gynaecological matters were not discussed in such technical detail and with such freedom at that time as they are now.

My dad was one of four siblings, and my mother one of six. One single stand-alone child may have seemed to them to be unfortunate. With hindsight I'm inclined to think that there's a lot to be said in favour of single-childhood. I do realise that that implies criticism of my parents, who only wanted the best for me. They decided to adopt. Though they had made many good friends in Belfast, they never felt that it was their home. So they decided to adopt in Dublin.

In Ireland, legal adoption is a relatively modern institution. The first statutory provisions permitting adoption did not come into force until the beginning of 1953. At the time when my parents visited Dublin to find a child it would seem that adoptive parents more or less stepped in to a mother-and-baby home or an orphanage and, from the infants on display, made their choice. There were some papers to sign and details to sort out.

In autumn 1946 Will and Lydia travelled to Dublin, bringing me with them. In the Bethany Home in Rathgar they chose their child. How *like* Lydia that she didn't go straight for a little robust newish roly-poly baby! Rosemary Elizabeth was eighteen months old, solemn-faced, sitting apart by herself, and she stole Lydia's heart. She suffered from eczema, and she had rickets; she had curly copper-red hair and huge blue eyes. Her development had been slow. She cried in the train all the way to Belfast. A group of friends who conveniently worked on the spot, among them my uncle Jim, Willie Gillespie and Doris McWilliams, had slipped out of their Great Northern Railway offices to welcome us on the platform.

My new sister was re-named Dorothy Anne. Dorothy means 'Gift of God'. 'Anne' in Anne of Green Gables was my mother's fictional heroine, and she had red hair.

Rosemary Elizabeth/Dorothy Anne was so different from us, my parents could not have chosen anybody more different. Her beautiful red hair simply invited nicknames, so she was Copper-knob, Ginger – shortened to Ginnie, and Ginner and Gin. Helga was the name she began to use in her late teens, when she began to reconstruct her identity.

As soon as Dorothy, from the beginning a committed fabulist, understood that she was adopted, she took control of the story of her earliest life, during the period before she came to us. One of her early adventures was when she lived in Africa, a story she stuck to. It gave her a significance far outstripping anything I could invent! And I sensed that our parents would be complete spoilsports if I came up with a tale like that. Dorothy had a sort of disreputable glamour; she got away with murder.

As she grew up and followed me to school in Belfast, I began to realise the responsibilities of an older sister. These included rushing to the kindergarten in answer to emergency calls for help by her teacher. These occurred when Dorothy's notion of how to spend the day didn't coincide with the teacher's. Meltdown in a little copper-knobbed girl, whose blue eyes were flooding with tears, and who *would not stop* crying at the top of her voice, was a challenge for which the teachers had not been trained.

The Drama Queen and a New Look

Even when she was very young, Dorothy had a taste for drama. With such a need for attention, you don't wait for drama to happen, you create it. When our Auntie from Dublin stayed with us, it was almost inevitable that Dorothy would find her pills, carefully stored in a safe place, and that she would gobble up a handful. She was in a coma for days, disappointingly missing the very real crisis that was swirling round her. I remember a quiet house, my parents preoccupied and worried. They had chosen to adopt Dorothy, and they had failed to keep her safe. The owner of the sleeping pills needed to be calmed and reassured. No doubt someone had to go to the pharmacy to get replacement pills, and the medicine was then tucked away, super-safely, maybe behind lock and key.

Life was full of interest. One day a little friend very foolishly swallowed a Pin. The doctor prescribed cotton-wool sandwiches as a remedy. There was a lot of fuss, and it was such a very unusual drama that Dorothy was inspired. She went for it. Wise girl didn't swallow a pin, but her story that she had done so, along with such honest blue eyes – 'mummy, I did, really and truly!' – resulted in a trip to hospital for a series of x-rays. I suppose she got a lecture, but it had been well worth it. Had I been her parent I would have made sure she didn't miss out on the full experience. She would have had her cotton-wool sandwich.

Floods of tears, shrieks and sobs, fear... My sister was still very young when she had to have her tonsils out. My parents brought her to the Benn Hospital. She screamed, the nurse firmly detached her from Lydia's arms, and my parents had to leave her there. I assume that the Benn was no different from some other hospitals in those days. I've read that they could be economical with anaesthetic, particularly in the case of straightforward procedures being performed speedily on young children. Provided the child didn't die, they would recover. They would forget the pain.

Apart from that, there was another reason for Dorothy to suffer from post-traumatic shock, after the experience in the Benn. It was advised by experts that parents should not visit their children in hospital, as visits upset the children, they cried when mother and father left. This disturbed the peaceful ward. Unvisited little ones may have cried briefly, but they gave that up and became quiet, which meant 'good', having learned that no mother and father came to comfort them. Will and Lydia were not allowed to visit. Such sorrow. Such cruelty.

Many hearts have been broken in Ireland over the years, and the excuse has been 'Ah, that was then. Things were different, it was the culture of the time'. That's an indictment on society, not an acceptable excuse for stony hearts.

My life was being enriched in different ways while all the Dorothy-dramas took place. Clothes began to be very interesting, ladies' clothes. Learning by observing, I appreciated elegance, line and colour; at that time the parts of an outfit matched, or in contrasting they went together. 'No, don't wear that, it doesn't go!' My mum dressed simply and with taste, and I loved the sound of her good, go-to-meeting shoes. They had cuban heels, which sounded like ponies' hooves, 'click, clack, clock, Clark!'

Once upon a time, nearly one hundred and ninety years ago, in the town of Street in Somerset lived Mr Clark. He worked as a tanner, making sheepskin rugs. One day he looked at the offcuts and had a brainwave. Slippers! Slippers were followed in time by shoes and sandals. Then Clark's shoes were made for ladies, some with excitingly high heels. The sound of them – onomatopoea in a shoe! A little girl's dreams were born. How long would I have to wait before I would be grown-up enough to 'walk in beauty' like Lord Byron's lady? Sadly, I showed few signs of developing the spiritual or personal beauty he describes. Nonetheless, a beautiful shoe is a beautiful shoe. We weren't a very well-heeled family, but I had a high-heeled mind.

Clark's did go through a period in the doldrums, but in 1941 the company was reinvigorated by a third generation Clark. The newly invigorated Clarks and I are the same age! That's worth celebrating. Suddenly, I need to buy a new pair of heels!

Another delight for me was the sudden impact on women's fashions of the New Look! After the war years, with their restrictive coupons and utilitarian clothing, rich fabric was available again – in quantity! – and Christian Dior met the challenge. He named his first collection the Carolle Line, but America called it the New Look. It featured women's clothes which nipped in the waist, hugged the body, and swung luxuriously almost to the ankle, extravagantly flaring. I was entranced by the full swirling skirts, the high heels, the dramatic hats.

On a bus one day, a lady – you couldn't call her a woman, she was a Lady – sat in a seat beside the central aisle. Her skirt fell from her tiny waist, over her knees and down over the side of the seat, in folds onto the floor beside her. I was riveted. The image has never left me. One day I would be grownup, and I would be like that. Dior's exquisite long narrow skirts didn't, at that time, do anything for me.

I had a new, different, experience which stunned me. I was brought to a concert, where I heard people singing in four-part harmony. I didn't know such a sound could exist! I wanted to hear it for ever, I wanted to eat it! I think I was running a temperature. And heaven would be better!

Fauré's 'Cantique de Jean Racine' just happens to be accompanying me as I type, and I'm five-years-old again, eyes wide, bewitched.

2
HOME

MY parents, particularly my mother, never felt fully at home in Belfast. The sense of being in exile never left them. I'm pretty sure that Will's and Lydia's prayers included a suggestion to God that it might be His will to return them to Dublin. It was His will. My dad accepted the position of Fire Manager in Dublin with the Shield Insurance Company.

In 1950 we packed our bags and we all came home. Dorothy was five, and I was nine.

Willingness to accept God's will was central to my parents lives. My mother fortified herself with prayer, which she called 'just chatting to God', and they both believed that God's choices were the best for them. My dad would explore the Bible, and approach sticky theological topics on the blind side while he explored truth. My mother said, quoting a Bible verse, 'As for God, His way is perfect'.

It does seem slightly ironic that a man whose life was committed to obedience to God should be called Will.

Dublin had real buses, rocky and noisy, with a wonderful growling whoosh from the engine as it picked up speed. Belfast trolley buses only hummed. The whoosh was the bus breathing. Sometimes it took so long to take a breath that I was worried. No automatic transmission then! The driver changed gear when he felt like it, never suspecting that a wee girl in his bus was holding her breath too.

We lived for a few weeks in Dollymount, North Dublin, in a borrowed house while we waited for our new one to be ready. For me the move was made glorious by our spending a night in a Hotel in Wicklow Street. It was impossibly glamorous. I had a peep at the delights that I could look forward to, when I grew up and had lots of money.

Glamorous, but in a different way, were the Nuns whom we often saw on the bus. The technical terms for their wonderful clothes were a *wimple* and a *habit*. The habit was a long heavy dress of robust deep blue fabric, belted, with a chain of beads hanging from the belt. This, I discovered later was a set of Rosary (what an exquisite word) Beads, with a little crucifix attached to it. But oh! the wimple! High white wings, sails, rose on each side from a starched coif, tilting, swaying, luminous, as these dedicated women moved gently through the city. Belfast, try to match that!

I went to school in Wesley College on St Stephen's Green. I was aged nine, and I was in the lowest form in the prep school, Prep C. It was the lowest class, with the newest pupils. With great joy, after nine long years spent creeping to school like a snail, I walked out for good! I remember every step of my leaving. In school we hadn't studied As You Like It, so I hadn't words to express my joy fully. If I had known the play, you might have seen me tripping joyously down the school driveway, past the school chapel on my left and the big Methodist church on my right, across the road into 'the Forest of Arden', chortling with Celia –

> 'O wonderful, wonderful, and most wonderful!
> And yet again wonderful, and after that, out of all whooping!'

George Bernard Shaw was a pupil of Wesley. It's said that he hated it. To be honest, it wasn't a bad place, lots of happy wholesome boys and girls probably loved it. GBS and I shared a hatred of being trapped. In school one was extremely trapped. He harboured a lifelong animosity towards schools as places of education and teachers, viewing them rather as prisons and turnkeys in which children are kept. He disliked being organised, and as a result, his education was irregular.

The building was ancient, nothing like Malory Towers, or the even more enchanting Whyteleafe School, in which Elizabeth was The Naughtiest Girl. Enid Blyton invented the first of these boarding schools in 1941, the year I was born. Perfect timing. My dad loved Whyteleafe, partly because it was democratically run, and also because it was co-ed. My parents were enthusiastic about co-education.

I can hardly believe that they chose to send me to Wesley College because of an Enid Blyton school story.

It was shabby and barren and noisy and full of gruff clattering boys, and alien girls, and staff in billowing black academic gowns, some of whom called me Miss Cochran. In the 1950s Wesley staff still addressed the boys by their surnames, and weirdly, the girls' surnames were preceded by Miss. Miss Cochran! I was just a child.

One male teacher enjoyed hitting the boys on their hands with the edge of the ruler. When violence was being done to a boy, one felt terribly threatened. It might be me next. So none of us could relax. He did hit me, once. I remember it.

Another minor incident scarred me for life. I offended the Geography teacher, and he decided to send me to detention, commanding me to 'write a note'. Since I had never been in detention before, I had no idea how to Write a Note, and I didn't know where detention happened. It felt like being told to dig my own grave blindfolded, without a shovel.

I found that I lived on the wrong side of town, too. I should have been housed in Rathgar, Terenure or Rathmines, anywhere on the South side. Dollymount was unheard of; even Clontarf, where we later settled, was a strange place to come from. They speak differently there.

The number 30 bus took me from Dollymount to Lower Abbey

Street in the city centre, and then I took a number 15 across the city to the school. Our friend Olive, living in Dublin now, was always available to cherish me. She met me for some weeks in town, and shepherded me between buses, and comforted me when a man made himself horridly unpleasant to me. (If this happened today, we would have screamed for the Garda, and the offender would have had his day in court, and possibly a sentence of five years, reduced to five days, suspended, because he had some educational or psychological issues.)

The trips back home after school were different on the days when I played hockey. When school ended at three o'clock, we walked in crocodile to the hockey pitch in the Leeson street area. When practice finished, I took a number 11 bus back into the city centre to catch the bus home. I once captained the Third Eleven, when I was about fourteen. We played at what was then Knockrabo, in Goatstown, miles into unknown territory. I was a bit late; bus difficulties. And I muffed being captain. At the close of the match I was too shy to shout 'Three cheers for ... School', when we were all supposed to wave our sticks in the air.

I had also temporarily forgotten the name of the school we'd beaten. Poor show. Not leadership material.

In due course we moved to our own new house at 28, Blackheath Gardens, Clontarf.

Lydia's gift for making friends is illustrated by a story. Beside us lived the O'Kelly family. After years of the two families living cheek by jowl, one day some family members were visiting next door. Later in the day an alarm was raised! The three-year-old granddaughter was missing. As our homes were in a cul de sac, there were no busy roads, and very few people passed by. There was intensive searching and great anxiety. Eventually Róisín was found, fast asleep, tucked up *in my parents' bed*. Her slippers were placed tidily together on the floor. Róisín's aunt Ita told me this story, commenting on how very much at home the little girl had felt in my parents' house.

> Let us think of a bad school. I mean a school where children sit at desks and speak when they are spoken to.
>
> **A.S Neill, founder of Summerhill School, attributed**

Now I took the number 44A bus from Seafield Road in place of the 30. In Prep C I was a microscopically small tiddler in a simply enormous ocean full of creatures, sharks and whales bigger and braver and more clever than I. I did not like it. I didn't know then that my sense of alienation reflected my actually being different. My Northern accent marked me out, and my tastes and interests didn't chime with those of the other children.

In first year in Wesley, subject choices were made.

I took Domestic Science (Home Ec.) and Latin, instead of Science and Commerce. Life-changing choices, but we hadn't a clue about the choices' possible significance. Maybe without the kick-start of Domestic Science I wouldn't have had the fun, and it's been such fun, of making my own and my sister's clothes from the age of thirteen, followed as the years passed by curtains, lampshades, quilts, wedding dresses – mine and my daughters' – bridesmaids' dresses, chair covers.

If it could be home-made, I made it. I used, and still use, the Singer sewing machine which my mother bought, second-hand probably, in 1942. It's worked by a windey handle. It looks beautiful, and it weighs an absolute ton. I don't say tonne, the machine's great age would have nothing to do with today's childishly simple metric measures.

Latin is wonderful, a mixture of maths and poetry, and I was hopeless at it, as usual not realising that I should study, instead just letting the beautiful precision of the sentences slither through my head and be lost. In spite of learning very little Latin, I found later delight in its presence in English, soaked as English is with Latin-based words and phrases. Later I learned a tiny bit of Greek, which enhanced my understanding of English as well. It was well worth the time spent sitting through the boring classes, and I didn't miss doing Commerce – well, I didn't know what it was, how could I miss it?

Oh, I would like to have studied Science.

My new piano teacher was Miss Foster, a short bike-ride from my home. She had a Golden Cocker Spaniel, and would wipe its teary eye with the silken fringe of a long ear. I lapsed into mediocre piano-playing, partly because I hardly ever practised. The days were too full, and my mother wasn't tough enough to compel me to do it. In truth, I was lazy.

We had a great family adventure soon after we settled in Dublin. For our summer holiday fortnight we went to a Guest House, Plas Menai, in Llanfairfechan, North Wales. It was a home from home for like-minded people from the UK and Ireland, and my mother became friends with most of them. I remember an evening concert of some sort, at which a blind woman sang a solo. Later, at bedtime my mother accompanied this lady to her room. After saying goodnight, Lydia said 'I'll leave the light on for you'. 'Oh, my dear' said the singer, 'you can turn it off. I don't need it'.

Subsequent to that holiday I announced grandiloquently that my favourite pastime was travelling.

In Dublin Will developed his latent interest in Homeopathy. He was intensely interested in exploring subjects that were unusual, new-fangled, exotic. He owned textbooks on maths, on Gardening without Digging, on Theology, on Greek and Hebrew, on Better Sight without Glasses, on the complexities of Insurance Broking and Statistics. There was an independence of mind that won him friends and respect, and made some people a bit wary of him. When he started courting Lydia, her family in Blessington found him challenging; they were Protestant 'West Brit' people, and Will identified himself as republican. There was a small 'r', to take the harm out of it, but he was quite proud that George Gilmore, very much a Republican, was a cousin a few times removed.

Speaking of courting, when my husband Keith first visited my parents' house, it was to find that Will loved to garden at night, illuminated by an electric light bulb on an extension cable hooked over a convenient branch or hook or the top of the ladder, and dressed for labouring in ancient flannel trousers and a battered tweed jacket with its fronts tied together with string. He always wore a jacket. For the pockets. Nobody had heard of Man-bags.

Homeopathy pleased him by its emphasis on the individual character of the client for whom the practitioner was making a diagnosis, and by the principle of 'the magic of the minimum dose' which informed the making and the prescribing of the remedies. Mr Roy Ogden was a well-known practitioner in Dublin, and my dad became friendly with him. Lydia's general health was not robust, and Mr Ogden began to prescribe for her. At the beginning of 1953 she became pregnant. She was thirty-nine.

I was eleven, and I don't remember feeling any curiosity about this development. I didn't wonder about any of the details of my mother's not-really-very-interesting condition, nor what caused it. I was pre-occupied with managing my own small challenges. My sister Dorothy was both a charming and a difficult child, who needed a great deal of attention.

At that time there was little or no support offered to people who adopted. My parents strove to give Dorothy all the advantages they had given to me. But her temperament and her gifts were completely different to mine. I think that the narrowly academic approach to education, which suited me, was not appropriate for her. It makes me happy to remember that when she grew up and left home, she was able to express herself with weaving and pottery, and mix with people who valued these crafts highly. My parents had no experience of different life-choices, in which someone could find fulfilment and joy in creative work, as a way of life. My father's mother had been an amateur musician and poet, but her gifts, while they made her four sons proud, don't seem to have added much substance to their experiences growing up. It was a male household, and perhaps Lizzy Cochran's undoubted gifts were viewed as being just female dabbling. The story was told that my paternal grandmother would sigh, saying 'I'd love a scone for tea' but it wouldn't occur to her to make one. When her third son married my mother, his life became scone-filled, and he loved them, every one.

At first Dorothy attended a small private school in Clontarf run by my music teacher, where she would, true to form, kick up a rumpus when something displeased her. The rumpus could be soothed by chocolate. The gifted dedicated teacher, Laura Foster, often resorted to chocolate therapy. There is a precedent for using that simple and direct means to restoring peace:

'I'm a good girl, I am. I've always been a good girl' cried Eliza.
Professor Higgins lost his patience,
'Pickering, give her a chocolate!'

George Bernard Shaw, Pygmalion

Since Miss Foster taught me piano, my parents – again giving Dorothy every advantage – asked her to teach my sister as well. I hope the fees stretched to buying lots of chocolate. Later Dorothy attended the Wesley College Junior School, called Tullamaine, on Leeson street, a terribly long journey from home. Her life became increasingly complicated as she grew up.

'One day I wrote her name upon the sand,
but came the waves and washed it away...'

Edmund Spenser

In her first 18 months of life, in Bethany Home, baby Rosemary Elizabeth may not have had consistent intimate parenting. She may have missed having a steady responsive relationship with one particular carer. The system in place in The Home was that after a baby was born, the mother stayed in Bethany. Would she have been encouraged to breast-feed the baby? The emotional bonding from that intimacy, which would sooner or later be ruptured by separation, might have been a reason for bottle-feeding being the norm. The mother was expected to get a job and go out to work to earn her living. Her baby was cared for during the day by the Staff. When a baby was adopted the mother would leave, to begin her new life, without her child.

Dorothy's mother, therefore, while continuing to live in Bethany, went out to work between 1945 and late 1946. She had previously worked as a Home Help for friends of my parents, in Dublin. As that was during our time in Belfast, I think my parents may never have met her. The mother and baby home was run with great commitment and with kindness, but certainly with too few staff, too little money, and with the prevailing no-nonsense attitude of the day. Some children, with calm equable temperaments and good health, overcame these disadvantages. Some did not.

When my parents chose Rosemary, they took her from her familiar place at a time when she was old enough to be aware of loss and confusion, but not old enough to understand what was happening. After the long train journey more strangers descended upon the exhausted little group. Even people who are besotted with all things railway can imagine the terror of that jolting noisy endless journey, hauled by a turbulent engine that now and again *shrieked.*

On her adoption, the girl-baby was given new names. Our parents believed that two daughters with the initials R.E. might in the future cause problems. So Rosemary Elizabeth became Dorothy Anne.

As she grew up, she became indiscriminately sociable, wanting to be friends and to form relationships with any and everybody. Psychologists today might use the sturdy phrase 'Reactive Attachment Disorder' to refer to Dorothy's way of coping with life. In 1946 such ideas never entered anybody's head. There was no person with experience and skill to offer advice. Will and Lydia were on their own. My mother, who greatly loved children, poured her heart and mind and will into nurturing this tiny girl, with prayers and tears.

On the 22nd November, 2006, just as I was preparing to visit Dorothy in Hampshire, England, I got a phone call from her partner to say that my sister had died.

3

THE BOY

IN early 1953 Lydia's close friend Doris Hodgins brought her newborn twins, Heather and Rodney, home from the Rotunda Hospital. Lydia went to visit her, and told Doris that she herself was pregnant.

The pregnancy was complicated. Lydia was frail, and she tended to faint. She toppled into the vegetable patch in our garden. She fainted at the bus stop when she and my dad were taking me into town, to play in a Feis Ceoil piano competition. It gave me an excuse for not winning. In fact there was not the slightest chance that I might win, even had I practised.

A maid, Peggy, came to live with us and help us, 'on loan' from friends. Maybe she was called a 'mother's help'? In Belfast my mother had been supported by Ellie, a 'charm-woman', more commonly called a 'char'. Ellie's dangling marcasite earrings gave me an unreasonable dislike of marcasite. But Peggy was beautiful. Her hair was a black cloud, and she had lovely pink-and-white colouring. I only remember her smiling.

Peggy was a horse-woman, and she had a horse stabled at Killester, not far away. She took me to visit it, and I was allowed to ride down Castle Avenue! I was twitching the reins, and she said to me, 'Ruth, don't play with his mouth'. I was actually learning to ride! Is there a young girl alive who wouldn't love that? My weekly comic, School Friend, which Olive bought for me, was full of Girls Who Rode – and now I was one of them!

Then, on a dark September night, my parents travelled to the Nursing Home in Baggot Street, and Michael was born. He was named John Gordon Cochran. John means 'God is Gracious'. Gordon had a 'nice strong sound'. We called him Gordon.

The birth was protracted.

Gordon weighed 5lb 5oz, a 'fragile little soul'. Will called him his five-guinea baby. He was sleepy and floppy. Feeding him was a long-drawn-out business as he could not stay awake, and he had no notion of sucking. Lydia remarked years later that they should have suspected that something was wrong, as this indifference to feeding was a recognised indicator of developmental problems.

Usually, young babies concentrate on doing two things, to varying degrees. They eat and they sleep. This little fellow didn't care for eating, and *he would not sleep*. His mother stood by the cot, and sang and sang her heart out.

As a family we didn't know much 'popular' music. We didn't listen to the radio, and our needs to hum and sing and whistle were met partly by the music we knew from my dad's piano playing, and partly by the hymns that we knew off by heart from church. So for a lullaby Lydia sang,

Jesus, tender Shepherd, hear me,
Bless Thy little lamb tonight;
Through the darkness be Thou near me,
Keep me safe till morning light.

To the tune Blaenwern

And she sang,

'Jesus loves me! This I know,
For the Bible tells me so;
Little ones to Him belong,
They are weak but He is strong'.

And she sang ,

> 'There's a Friend for little children, above the bright blue sky.
> A friend who never changes, whose love will never die...'

One evening I did a little test. I noted on the piano where my mum's singing was pitched, and now and then I checked to see how she was doing. During the half-hour or so, her voice stayed true. She never slipped in pitch, though she was so tired, and half asleep herself. Perfect pitch, on auto-pilot.

When Gordon was big enough to be brought to church, it was his pleasure to sing. Not the hymn of the moment, but a sort of generic melody that suited all the hymns, and hearing his joyful noise made some people very happy. Lacking any real words, in time Gordon vocalised his understanding of what church was about, by calling it Lah-lah.

Though in our house we didn't hear any pre-pop Popular Music, I do have a charming memory of my Auntie Essie doing her George Formby turn, singing,

> 'I'm leaning on a lamp-post at the corner of the street,
> In case a certain little lady passes by. Oh me, oh my...'

Lydia's years of bed-time singing to Gordon weren't wasted. Nor was her tender nurturing of Dorothy. Nor were my dad's patient night-time responses to my yells, when I was small. Such love in action isn't wasted. Hearing Lydia giving herself in song to her boy, I learned that being patient is something you decide to practise. It's something you choose to do, even when – particularly when – you don't feel like it.

A visiting friend recognised that there was a problem; the tiny boy just couldn't be bothered doing what should have been instinctive. Friend Doris confided her early misgivings to Lydia's sister-in-law, who counselled caution – *'don't say anything to Lydia!'*

I remember my mother touching his bare tummy with the chilly talcum-powder tin to wake him up to feed. At a time when other babies were slinging toys out of the pram, or trying to climb out, Gordon lay passive. His soft hands were always cold, and I used to hold them in mine and 'pet' them and say tenderly to him 'darling, your tiny hands are frozen'. I loved him with my whole heart.

The Dedication

My parents prayed for their new boy. My father's deliberate, considered prayer, characteristic of his faith in God, and of his hopes for his son, was that *Gordon would grow up to be a great preacher of the Gospel.*

God said 'Yes, I hear your prayer, and I will do what you ask. Just wait a little while and watch me do it!'

Will didn't know what he meant by his prayer. He didn't suggest how God might achieve such an unlikely outcome for Gordon. But it was worth trying, and praying was what Will did best.

Gordon's development was slow, and within months it was clear to everybody that he wasn't developing normally. I didn't know much about the consultations and discussions that took place, with doctors and specialists. After some time my dad told me that the doctors believed Gordon to be slightly 'Mongoloid', the condition which is now called Down Syndrome. One indicator of the disorder apparently was his distinctively formed hands. I don't think that one can have 'slight' Down Syndrome, or that any such random diagnosis would be made today. Baldly, he was brain-damaged, due to oxygen deprivation because of a dysfunctional placenta. Hypoxic brain injury, in a nutshell.

This was the first time that I heard anyone saying that Gordon was not 'normal'. This was a bad thing. Our brother had been physically and mentally injured, his body was disabled, and his brain was disabled. He was surely doomed. I felt a new thing, a cold icy stone settling in my tummy. What about Dorothy's and my dreams about our lively fun-loving brother? We had planned that he would be strong and clever, a king among boys. I sensed that we were moving into a literally un-thinkable situation. A grey cloud which threatened disappointment and sorrow settled over me. Our father and mother, frighteningly, couldn't make it go away.

I had to let go my anticipation of this brother growing into a jolly rumbustious chum. Instead, in place of that fantasy boy, we had the sweetest softest little cuddly treasure. I didn't know what sort of future he would have. *Try not to think. He's a darling, now.*

There are some things that I know, with hindsight. My parents protected Dorothy and me from sorrow and worry as much as they could. Because of that we missed a lot of what they were experiencing. But I believe it was lonely for me, and confusing for Dorothy. Would the icy lump of anxiety in my tummy have melted if we could have talked about the trouble? I could have asked questions. Would my mum and dad have risked telling me that they were sad and perplexed? Would they have dared to risk crying with me?

Looking back, I think that the weight in my tummy was partly unconscious worry about my parents. That was destabilising me. It was shaking my foundations. They were under some sort of attack, and I couldn't make it better for them, or protect them, or keep myself and Dorothy safe.

I wasn't admitted into their confidence, nor was I reassured that it was all right. I survived. Later, in my own parenting, I didn't always get it right either.

At twelve years old I was struggling as usual with the challenges of school life. But I know that since Gordon was born, a little fubsy boy, I have most tenderly loved babies, and been enchanted by their simplicity and their mystery.

There was the ache in my tummy. Family life was changed, and would stay changed. No return.

In her diary Lydia wrote,

> Gordon born. So tiny. Future unknown, joy and trusting.

Lydia's oldest brother, Jim, still lived in Belfast. He was prosperous, involved with voluntary organisations for people with disabilities, and when Gordon was still very young, Uncle Jim realised that there was a problem. He advised my parents to go for specialised medical help. He suggested to them that he would help them to place Gordon in a residential home, in Craigavad in Northern Ireland, and he would take full responsibility for him. This place was one of many, worldwide, founded and run on the principles of the Austrian philosopher and social reformer, Rudolf Steiner.

Steiner's adventurous thinking encompassed anthroposophy, esotericism, mysticism, and his schools used art, music, poetry and handwork to encourage the whole-person development of the young child. From many perspectives it was an attractive offer, wonderfully generous, and the notion of a small Mentally Handicapped person being safe there, benevolently cared for, would have provoked serious thought. Family and friends were concerned for Will and Lydia; as a family we did seem to be under some pressure. Other people also advised putting Gordon into care, as was the practice of the day. In general one didn't see 'mentally handicapped' people mixing socially in public.

My parents never considered tidying Gordon away, not for a split second. If God had a purpose in allowing them to have this unique son, this little floppy fellow, his purpose would be best served by their holding on to the boy.

The Support Team

Years later my mother told me that she had never asked God 'Why?

The 'diary' in which Lydia wrote wasn't actually a Diary. It was a book written in 1925 by Mrs Chas. E. Cowman, called Streams in the Desert. Mrs Cowman compiled Bible readings for each day of the year, just a verse or a phrase. She followed these with comments taken from her own life, as a missionary with her husband in Japan and Korea, and then at home in California. The writer included extracts from other Christian writers, and verses of poetry.

The book echoes the old English of the King James Bible, and would seem archaic to a new reader today. But written in the margins, in almost every space, are my mother's comments on life, written as she read through each day, turning back to start again at the beginning as the year ended.

She wrote, and underlined, in the front of the book:

> Lydia Cochran. Given to me by my dear friend Ruth Heard at a time of great distress. The marks and underlinings are made because I have been reproved and blessed, by all the Lord's dealings with me – always in love and tenderness.

Lydia's brother Jim, and Will's brother Sam, as well as many friends, were supportive, not just with love and friendship, but with significant gifts of money. Will's salary wasn't large; he never seemed to get the hang of making money. I didn't know anything about the support they received at the time, but I felt the effect, and I loved both the uncles, so much.

Housekeeping was hard work. Lydia needed to use her energy wisely, so she took every shortcut she could. When guests were expected Dorothy or I would be sent upstairs to 'pick the bits off the landing carpet'. It was an oddly designed upstairs, with a long landing, and since the only loo was upstairs at the far end of the passage, the carpet needed to be presentable.

The nearest grocery shops were a twenty-minute walk away, uphill. But that was no problem. Lydia phoned her orders to our neighbour, Alf, who had a shop in Marino, and he brought everything up at lunchtime. She phoned the butcher, asking for 'half a pound of lean round steak please, and four gigot chops.'

Barney, the Kennedy's breadman came to the door. I remember Bermaline was a gentle brown loaf, not rough, as were some of other brown ones. Kennedy's shop was in Killester, the floury warm smell drawing people in. Did anybody ever come in just to stand in the wide yeasty space, and breathe?

Other life-savers called to the house on spec, including the Cake Man, from a bakery in Sutton. We bought the Malt Loaf, a change from scones. The Fish Man came, the Vegetable Man, the Laundry Man, who returned with the precisely folded ironed bed linen. My mother's support team. I remember Barney, and I can picture him clearly, also Alf who kept us in groceries.

Friendship

'Isn't Beethoven *jolly*?' said Aileen, who is my second cousin once removed, one day long after I had grown up. I visit her every now and then and she gives me lunch and we talk about everything under the sun. One day our conversation came back to music, which we both love. She lit the conversation up with this unexpected but perfectly apt question. Yes Beethoven is jolly! It's the special way that people who are fighting and winning life's battles can lightheartedly chuckle and joyfully joke.

When I was in my teens Aileen sometimes invited me to visit her lovely old villa on the Clontarf Road, and she played for me recordings of music. Time stopped and I relaxed. On these occasions, as well as being soothed by music and friendship, I felt very mature, part of a cultured adult world. I admired Aileen enormously; she was clever, and independent, and musical, and a committed Christian, whom I could wholeheartedly try to emulate.

Aileen's elderly parents, George and Nell, were kind – and brave. They recklessly used to invite us all for tea. As guests, we were a fairly challenging family. Gordon was unpredictable, and it didn't take much to provoke outbursts of frustration as he grew out of toddler years. Baby tantrums were followed by confrontation, as, unable to say – or explain – what he felt, he was often destructive or violent.

My mother's sister Essie, (every name of that generation was abbreviated, as in the siblings, Jim, Harry, Charlie, Lyddy, Willie, Essie) was a weekly visitor to our home, and she was so good to me. She took me cycling to Malahide. Her particular passion was fine 'nylons', stockings which were impractical wisps of luxurious gossamer. I remember she had a dress in crêpe with tiny flowers, a 'tea-dress', which I admired. Those lovely clothes set another grown-up standard that I felt sure would become mine.

Essie was one of the people, close to my parents, whose hearts were wrenched by the pickle Lydia and Will found themselves in, with their pesky children. Some of those friends were personally very kind to me and to Dorothy. Others helped by giving money to my parents; there were women who held Lydia steady, men who showed practical and spiritual fellowship to Will.

My parents' friends and family are significant in this story, their grace and lovingkindness can't be measured. The outcome after many years has been that I inherited some of these friends after my parents died. I am blessed.

I've mentioned Olive Nelson. She was a single lady, with a fine career. She cared for her mother and her sisters and brothers in turn as they needed it. She loved children. She loved her nieces and nephews, and her friends' children, and those in her church, for whom for years she ran a children's club.

Olive had a central place in Gordon's story, for me. The gladness of her smile, when she arrived and hugged me. She pet-named me Shuthers, and lifted my heart and smoothed the tangles in my mind. Life seemed simpler; I relaxed. She gave me books to read, she took me for treats, she taught me to swim, she brought surprises to me at a time when I was ill and off school for a whole term!

However, though Olive was able to smooth my tangled mind, she was not at all good at coping with other tangles. When she lived with us in Belfast it was her pleasure to get me ready for the day. My hair was long and ringletty, and needed to be thoroughly brushed before being braided into two plaits. I stood in the big kitchen while Olive, chatting with my mum, gently brushed the *surface* of my hair, softly and absent-mindedly, and then she began to make plaits. It was torture. Plait torture for other children might be because the braiding was too tight. I would have welcomed that. Olive chatted on, to my mum or to me, and the plaits got looser and looser, and I became restive, irritated, then frantic, until one day I exploded, 'You're a jacky old Auntie Olive, and you're not even married!'

People like this helped my parents to cope.

One Dublin ritual I remember with nostalgia was the Wednesday afternoon visits we paid to my mother's friend Lucy. We walked up Castle Avenue to Lucy and Henry's bungalow. I would be settled in the beautiful drawing-room, with some titbits to eat, and the current 'Woman's Weekly' magazine to read. The others had their afternoon tea in the breakfast room! The idea was to give me a bit of peace, to which apparently I was entitled.

I adored that magazine. The fashion articles, by 'The London Girl', were illustrated by drawings which I admired very much, and tried to copy. In photos the models wore smart outfits, in toning colours. My dress sense was further formed, on the way to school in my teens, by the windows of Alys Glennon's shop, at the top of Dawson Street. The bus to school went up Dawson Street, and as it paused before turning right I daily feasted my eyes on dreamily coloured tweed skirts and jackets, delicate blouses and finest woollens. All the shades in harmony, complemented by the most desirable accessories. Ten years later I found that some of my young husband's relations actually bought Alys Glennon's clothes! In my school days I never imagined I would have such lofty in-laws.

The two 'Mills & Boon' serial stories in Woman's Weekly fed my idealistic romantic yearnings. The love stories were of the mildest; I understand that today's Mills & Boon stories are very different. They did me no harm at all, though I believe some, gently-raised, conservative acquaintances of Lydia's raised their eyebrows. School Friend and Woman's Weekly in tandem gave me two contrasting, and very welcome, avenues of escape.

Just Being Children

Round and round we dashed, faster and faster, until we collapsed helpless onto the floor. In our house, the first door on the left of the hall led into the drawing room. The second door, just beyond it, led into the dining room. Between the two rooms were sliding doors, which were always open. So you could walk into the first room, curl round to the right into the second room, and complete the circle back into the hall.

Dorothy and I would chase each other around this tight circle, shrieking and doubling back, to crash together in utter panic. It was the best fun, flying through the doorways, trying to catch each other, terrified, each knowing that if the other one suddenly doubled back *we would die*!

'Let's play Pam and Syv!'

Pamela and Sylvia were young women who lived in London, and worked in offices, and had lives of glamour and big salaries and beautiful clothes. They also, I suppose, had boyfriends. Dorothy and I regularly left the real world, and became Pam & Syv. Since I was the older one, I think that it was I who invented the game, inspired by 'The London Girl' in Women's Weekly. My sister enthusiastically joined in, using her imaginative gifts to embellish the storylines. It was pure escape, into a world where Dorothy and I could be who we wanted to be, and could make serious grown-up decisions without any concern about the outcomes. Oddly, I can't remember any romances we had. We were able to live in freedom in our perfect adult world. We could have as many friends as we liked – or as few. For those short times we lived, as equals, together.

Around the age of twelve, I was struggling with becoming a teenager. I was a picky, perfectionist child. As my sister Dorothy grew older, her character proved to be the opposite of all that was familiar to us, first of all mystifying our parents, and then exasperating her school-teachers, ultimately infuriating her employers. We played games together, and we were probably fond of each other, but oh, how we fought! She knew precisely how to drive me crazy, often to violence. We fought literally, of course, tooth and nail, and hair.

Add Gordon to the mix. Lydia was the home-maker, and the child-carer. Will was in full-time work. He often worked late into the evening. Insurance was a big part of my dad's life; it fascinated him, the mathematics, the statistics and the science of it. He was a distinguished Fellow of the Chartered Insurance Institute, and if circumstances had been more favourable he would have spent all day discussing the theory and the principles and practice of insurance, and all night labouring to do the work that earned his living. Because he had a dependent wife and three children, he couldn't stay out all night, so in the evenings he came home.

On Wednesdays he would go to the church prayer meeting. He also for a time went weekly to an early-morning prayer meeting, at which sometimes he was, ironically, the only human person present. He loved my mother deeply and completely. He loved his assorted children, but he was out of the home a very great deal. My mother was loyal and loving, she knew – thought? – that he was perfect. I do believe now that he found it very hard to cope with some of the challenges of home life. With Dorothy and with Gordon he was occasionally angry, in a frustrated heart-broken sort of way. Not with me. I was just an ordinary kid who was hot-tempered, shy, critical, untidy, lazy ... no problems there. Because I was bright, Will had dreams for me, involving academic excellence and, vaguely, some sort of success.

Baby Steps

Gordon walked. It took him a while. He was three before he began to get the hang of it. Carting him around was a weary business for Lydia. I did a fair bit of carrying, and loved the feel of him. The little fellow was very soft and squashy, his face a bit dreamy, with incurious quiet eyes. However, he learned to walk. Well, to toddle.

After some time, toilet training began. Even for the brightest and most co-operative children (and those two characteristics don't necessarily go hand-in-hand) potty training has its ups and downs. Gordon had only sisters as role models, and careful explanations about doing it standing up didn't inspire him. Dad was full of goodwill on this matter, but you need to be there, and he mostly wasn't. Lydia called for help from her best friend, who had a uniquely appropriate resource.

Doris came to the rescue. Her boy-twin, Rodney, was the same age as Gordon. So Rodney and Gordon were ushered into the back garden so that Rodney could demonstrate to Gordon how men do it. It worked.

In spite of Will having to be absent so much, which was normal then – Father going out to grapple with the world, and Mother staying at home to battle with the children – Gordon simply adored his dad. Well, why wouldn't he? Will was lovely, good-looking, funny, jokey, with the most beautiful eyes and a voice of great sweetness. The trouble was that the beautiful voice wasn't unique to him. Gordon was in his high-chair one day when Will's brother Sam arrived unannounced, and Gordon heard his voice in the hall. Joy unbounded! Dada's home! Followed by bitter inconsolable tears.

One day Lydia was ill. When this happened I usually stayed at home from school to care for Gordon. Dorothy went to school, because she was the younger one. She would have dearly loved to stay away from school. Sometimes Will was able to take time off work. On this particular day he had to go to a meeting, and it's probable that Dorothy and I had already left the house to scurry round to catch the bus to school. This was, however, an emergency, and Will was good in emergencies.

He phoned Doris, the steadfast friend, and made arrangements. He packed Gordon and himself into a taxi (we didn't have a car), and set off for Artane, where he would deliver his boy into Doris's care. He would then continue to his meeting. All nice and tidy. I never knew what was wrong with Lydia; she was quite often unwell, and managing us all really stretched her limited physical resources.

When Will and Gordon arrived at Doris's house they found that her mother, Mrs McWilliams, was visiting. She made friends with the little dreamy chap, and took him into the back garden to look at the birds. She had been a schoolteacher, and she loved to teach. After quite a frustrating time, with an unresponsive Gordon, grandmother brought him back into the house. 'This child can't see', she announced.

It was discovered that his sight was very bad. He got spectacles with thick plastic lenses. They didn't improve his vision much, because they were rarely on his nose. Well, would you wear glasses if you had a choice? Gordon struggled long and long, taking the specs off and hurling them upstairs and downstairs ... into the garden, onto the street, down the loo. It took patience, persistence, probably bribery, maybe little gentle threats? Anyway, I can confirm that he eventually accepted them.

About fifty years later, when his glasses still had thick lenses, one eye was operated on to remove a cataract. After that he wore glasses with one thick and one thin lens. It looked comical, but what progress! Mr Harold Melville, who was an optician, was a close friend of my parents, and he had a part in providing Gordon with the first specs, and quite probably in helping to organise endless repair jobs after Gordon had been heavy-handed yet again.

We never had much money. Will still didn't make money easily. Final Notices came through the letter-box, terrorising Lydia, but not ruffling Will's calm. We didn't go for two weeks' holiday to a seaside hotel. Friends occasionally lent us somewhere to stay for a week. However, no amount of money would have made conventional holidays, with Gordon in tow, easy to manage, unless we could have taken over a whole hotel, with staff.

So Will hired cars and we went out for trips. My beloved father, regarded as being intellectually brilliant, wasn't easy with mechanical things. He would read the instruction book, learn up all the unnecessary stuff, gather together some tools, put on a very old tweed jacket, tying it shut with its bit of string and, making sure there were no interruptions, attack the job.

Thus it was with driving. He would be a bit tense. So would we.

We went to the beach, Portmarnock, Donabate, or the Claremont beach at Howth. My mother didn't swim, having got a bad fright when, living in Belfast, she developed an embolism and was stuck in bed for a long time. Fear of another embolism incident, occurring when she was in the sea, kept her out of the sea for the rest of her life. Will had never, I think, actually been in the sea. It was alien to him; his preference was to be on it, in a boat. Traditionally, boatmen didn't want to learn to swim, as, if they were tipped into the sea, and then swam, the inevitable death would be long-drawn-out, a nightmare. To those who couldn't swim, death was presumed to be quick and merciful. Probably fishermen never put a toe into the sea, in case they might learn to swim by mistake.

One day we went to the beach, parking the car right beside the sand, where we spread out our towels. Dorothy and I got our togs on and went down to paddle. I glanced back just as, from behind the car, there appeared an apparition. It was tall and milk-white, with a baggy garment halfway down, and on top of it was my dad's head! That sweet man had bought a swimsuit, and he was coming to play with us and to keep us safe in the sea.

A Dog's Best Friend

'Would you like a puppy?' Would I what? In school, one of my friends was Diana. Her family dog produced puppies, and one of them was given to us. The pup grew to look like a small black Labrador Retriever, but while his looks may have been benignly Lab, his brain, inherited from a rogue ancestor, was pure Kerry Blue. In his book 'D is for Dogs', the late Frank Manolson says this:

> 'I've never met a Kerry Blue that wasn't a real character... take

> them in hand and start training early...enthusiasts maintain they're marvellous with children, but I've known several which couldn't be trusted not to injure themselves...don't be dissuaded from getting one...train it, and you'll have a superb pet'.

We named the puppy Bundle, after the black spaniel in Enid Blyton's The Family at Red-roofs. Before long he became Bundy, then for Gordon he was Bun-a-bun. Small Gordon toddled around in safety, shadowed by Bundy, his companion. As Gordon's pet, the dog was superb. As a dog, he was a pest. He fought with other dogs, he was ill with fits, he had fits when he was well, he got lost, and was found, and we loved him. Often it was I who intervened in these dramas. When he had fits I locked him in the garage, where he raced around yowling. I separated him from dogs which he wanted to kill. I went on my bike with my dad to search the neighbourhood when he was lost.

4

DUBLIN CAN BE HEAVEN

Lydia wouldn't have been able to drive, even if we had had a car. She was one of the least technically-minded people I've ever met. I don't think she ever opened a car door in her life. So when Lydia wanted to go to town, it was on the 44A bus, with Ruth, Dorothy and Gordon. My mother would carry Gordon on to the bus because of his delayed walking, giving Dorothy her bags to carry. I would fold up the 'go-car'.

This bulky chariot was the precursor of the push-chair and the buggy and today's stroller. I would lug it onto the open platform at the back, and wedge it into the stairwell, so that it wouldn't suddenly crash off when we went round a corner. Our model's wheels were wonky, you had to push it a bit sideways for it to go straight ahead.

My mother adored Dublin Town. When she was growing up, her home place, Blessington, was just a small village in the depths of County Wicklow. Lydia and her best friend Gladys Miller, who was nicknamed 'La', agreed that they would never, ever, consider marrying a farmer. La married a lovely countryman, Jack Byrne, and remained a countrywoman. Lydia shook the dust of country life off her feet, went to Dublin to work, became a city person, and married Will, whom she both admired and adored. Throughout her diary notes Will is referred to as Beloved and Binques. That name was derived from a family pet name, Bing; somewhere along the way it was changed and given the exotic spelling – I'm pretty sure that was done by Will himself. I never heard her call him by his 'proper' name.

So, we went to town. After he had grown up a bit, whatever Gordon planned to do in town had to be left till last, as, the moment his desires were granted, he needed to go home. How could you go to town again and again if you didn't go home quickly to plan the next trip? All his life long, Gordon planned and travelled and arrived. Whereupon, without delay, he planned the return journey. If that journey was delayed, he showed his concern by looking repeatedly at his watch, every two or three minutes. He could express urgency and impatience better that anyone I knew, and he was tireless. He could never willingly just hang around.

Bewley's Oriental Café in Grafton Street, was paradise. A plate of sausages-and-chips was a banquet. Lydia always asked that the sausages would be well-cooked, so that Gordon wouldn't be poisoned; then she checked with the waitress who brought the food to our table, 'Are the sausages well-done?' No waitress ever assured her that they tasted better half-raw. At home, our sausages would always be well brussed, so we never got food poisoning.

I wonder now how we coped with the stand of assorted buns and cakes, and the luscious butter, that stood all day on the tables. Surely we children wanted to wade into them and gobble the lot? Well, Gordon did make straight for the butter-balls! He was, after all, my butter-loving brother. The waitress's uniform of black dress, tiny white apron and white pleated headband was very pleasing to me. Maybe I was reminded of the nurses I had glimpsed in Belfast, when the bus passed a hospital, and the women in their pristine uniforms – symbols to me of their heavenly dedication – could be seen going about their business. Remembering the beautifully coiffed nuns, I did seem to have a bit of a thing about women in uniform.

When we were in Bewley's did the young waitress, 'Tattins' Twomey, ever serve us? She would have had a flower on her uniform dress, and with her sparkling dark eyes and special smile, it was her delight to attend to the groups of businessmen who met for coffee. Around mid-morning, that part of Bewley's became a gentlemen's club, and Tattins was the hostess who looked after the special guests.

We visited Pim's Department Store on Georges street, where Lydia's cousin Miss Ivers worked in Ladies Underwear. That was before the days when Ladies Underwear was poshed up to 'Longjeray'. Miss Ivers' generous embonpoint subtly supported the excellent reputation her department enjoyed.

On Christmas Eve we went to town as family to see the lights in Henry Street, where we were exhorted to buy the jumpin' jollies and the decoratin' chayens. Then we crossed town to have tea in Roberts at the top of Grafton Street. That was before Gay Byrne made the top of Grafton Street his own Christmas Eve patch. Just as well, really, as Gordon had a way of wading in to shake hands with whoever caught his fancy, and he would have been magnetically drawn to Gaybo. Startled revellers would have been greeted by Mr Byrne's new associate, shaking hands with gusto and wishing them, unintelligibly but unmistakably, Happy Christmas.

As a young man Gordon fell in love with another supremely Christmassy joy.

The Habits of Christmas – Let's Hear The Hallelujah Chorus!

Handel would be surprised if he could have seen the way his oratorio Messiah took on a life of its own after he composed it, more than two and a half centuries ago. It took him just twenty-four days to compose the music. The combination of the ravishing score, with a libretto telling the story of Jesus the Messiah taken from the Bible, enchanted its hearers. Since its first performance, in Dublin in 1742, it has been sung worldwide by almost everybody who could carry a tune, by Parish choirs with everybody doing their best, by music societies, by college choral groups with organ accompaniment, and in big professional productions with full orchestra and celebrity soloists.

Love for Messiah knows no boundaries! Gordon fell headlong in love with the oratorio on first hearing. Later, there was more Christmas jubilation when the Messiah Habit was joined by the Cathedral Christmas Carol Habit.

When Gordon was a teenager, his parents took him to hear his first Messiah, in Adelaide Road Presbyterian Church, in Dublin. Choirmaster Molly Dunlop's Trostan Singers didn't know, none of them ever learned, what a life-changing experience they were about to give to a unique and enchanted young man.

Because at home he lived with classical music, Gordon's ear wasn't tuned to pop. So he was happy and at ease sitting between his parents on the gallery, letting Messiah flow over him. Until, suddenly, without warning, the choir burst explosively into *Hallelujah! Hallelujah!*

The Hallelujahs soared, the music was transcendent, Gordon was entranced, and all over the hall people began to stand up!

Shivering with excitement, Gordon rose to his feet. His face was flaming, and his smile was so wide the top of his head might have flown off. He never got over it.

He went to lots of Messiahs. Now that he knew the drill, he was first on his feet for Hallelujah!

Helpfully, he took responsibility for actively encouraging shy or lazy audience members around him to do the right thing, to Stand Up!

Hallelujah, for the Lord our God Omnipotent reigneth.
The Kingdom of this world is become the
Kingdom of our Lord and of His Christ;
and He shall reign for ever and ever,
King of Kings, and Lord of Lords.

Revelation 11:15

Carol services were delightful too. Christmas music recitals would include carols and pieces from Messiah. Often they were in big churches, with galleries, but far outshining those quite lovely venues, there were Cathedrals!

Cathedrals are for Christmas. To lots of Dubliners St Patrick's Cathedral, in the middle of Old Dublin, is for carols. When Gordon was grown-up, I brought him to a service of Christmas music on a Christmas Sunday. Walking towards St Patrick's in the dusk, we were thrilled and deafened by the mad romping din of the bells. The cathedral was packed. I chose seats for us in the Nave, just beside the central aisle. Gordon always tended to occupy a seat very fully, with his arms and legs akimbo, so to place him in an aisle-side seat meant that he would have more space.

If he crowded me, I could poke him in the ribs.

Music swelled, and the choir and clergy procession entered at the back and began to come, slowly, slowly, up the aisle. Surplices, copes, stoles, frills, colour, measured pacing – Gordon had never in his life seen such splendour. The choir sang as they came level with us, almost touching Gordon, who was vibrating, completely starstruck. At the front, the boys and men took their places, and the congregation rose for the first carol. Gordon, needing space to sing his best, moved out into the aisle.

Congregations in that sort of church are usually quite tentative singers. The church singing that Gordon was used to was whole-hearted and unselfconscious. So, delighted to have a good crowd and a stunning environment, he swelled his chest and gave it his all. His voice was rich and mellow, and the words, and adherence to the beautiful melodies, didn't really matter much. I looked the other way.

Though he can't speak in the conventional sense, my brother likes to express himself, so when we were sitting down, listening, there were little mutterings, sotto voce hums and haws, the occasional private chuckle.

When it was over, the choir and the churchmen began to come down the aisle with great stateliness, singing. Gordon noticed a gorgeously surpliced man who seemed to be the most senior one. He kept his eye on him.

As the final members of the procession passed, Gordon stepped out into the aisle. The back of the cathedral was filling up with choir members, clergy, church officers and members of the congregation, in a civilised jumble of people moving in all directions. My brother focused on his target, the Dean, who was standing by the door, shaking hands and greeting friends with calm grace. Relentless, unstoppable, Gordon thrust his way through the throng towards the only person who really mattered.

The Dean found himself facing a little bespectacled man, whose face gleamed with joyful goodwill, and who was holding out a knobbly hand in brotherhood. They shook hands. Gordon murmured friendly things, and the Dean responded with great kindness.

A Lifelong Passion

Trips into Dublin Town confirmed in Gordon's young mind that buses were the best way to go anywhere. He adored travelling by bus. Later, he would be entranced by the glamour of train travel. To spend a day combining a bus journey with a trip on a train was a double joy. It was, however, serious business, never to be thought of as fun.

His great love was to travel, that is to go from one place to another. He was, after all, my kid brother. I had discovered the joy of travelling when I was taken 'abroad' to Wales. That wasn't very far, we only went across the water to the next bit of land. You could swim to Holyhead, if you had time, and practised. While Gordon's early travels were purely domestic, none of us could have guessed that, when he grew up, he would travel to places his parents never knew, and have adventures that they could not have dreamed of.

In the 1950's, businessmen could escape from the deadly grind of their offices and nip outside to drink morning coffee with their exhausted friends. Presumably they were expected to network, to make contacts, nod and wink over deals. A sort of 30-minute round of golf, but cheaper. Around mid-morning, when Gordon took his place in Bewleys with his mother and sisters, the gentlemen were at their tables. He glanced at them and then watched them attentively, scrutinised them. He recognised kindred spirits; these men were cut from the same cloth as were he and his father, but there was something tragically wrong.

Along with their wise sophisticated conversation, *they all had newspapers*, and he had none.

Could a boy with a fairly severe intellectual disability dedicate all the days of his life to the acquisition of newspapers? He could. Gordon did. He bought them when he had money, he stole them when he hadn't, he borrowed them, he helped the bus and train operators by taking away the newspapers which careless passengers left behind. Now and then there was a special prize, when he found a pink Financial Times that some irresponsible banker had dumped. Family members and friends discovered to their surprise that the newspapers that they thought they owned had become Gordon's possessions, as of right.

One day when Gordon was out and about with his mum, a kind newsvendor offered him an outdated newspaper. Ok, Gordon couldn't speak and he couldn't read, but he knew when he was being diddled, and he scornfully handed back the paper.

There was a delightful incident in Bewleys. A businessman was reading his Irish Times while having morning coffee. He laid it down for a minute to relax. He was astonished when a small young gent, with thick glasses and a certain air, stepped over and lifted the paper. Rather than nicking it, Gordon spread it out, folded it immaculately and returned it to its astounded owner.

A Taste for Business

As Gordon grew and learned to walk, and had life-changing experiences with buses and newspapers, he enjoyed having the run of his home, which meant access to the bedrooms, and also to my father's room at the end of the landing. This room, the fourth bedroom, was used by Will as his study. Well, he didn't actually study there, rather it was where he kept his business and church-related and personal papers, files, folders, heaps and boxes. These were connected with every department of his life; his work in insurance, household documents, books and other materials to do with his church life, and his writing and studying resources.

Many years later, I was able to explore the heaps and piles and folders of my dad's papers. They included bundles of letters received, and carbon copies of his replies, hand-written of course. It gave me an insight into areas of his life that I had known nothing about.

It also confirmed to me that our father knew absolutely nothing of the singular beauty of a dedicated filing system.

My little brother, having learned to walk, realised that it brought delightful freedom. That room, Will's study, was also where our aunt slept on her weekly visits. She was trustworthy; my parents were happy that the papers would of course be safe with her.

They underestimated Gordon. He had already started to admire his father's lifestyle as a businessman, the most exalted position a man could hold, in the view of one little boy. Businessmen do their work with Documents, which were gloriously crisp, foldable, important things, covered in intriguing print. They lived in Briefcases. Later he realised that you can't have one without the other; an armful of loose papers is just as distressing as an empty briefcase.

But before Gordon reached the briefcase stage, he practised the acquisition and management of as much paperwork as he could lay his hands on. Since nobody actually sent him sheaves of letters in the post, he stole whatever, whenever, he could. It was the beginning of a lifetime of dedicated document theft.

Therefore Will locked the door of his 'study', and Lydia loyally kept it locked, and Essie guarded the documents when she slept there. And nobody knew how it was that Gordon managed to get his hands on them, but now and then he circumvented the guardians of the treasures, and was found to have some of Will's letters or financial statements in his small grubby hands.

He learned to write his name, and he couldn't help writing it on everything he stole. The other thing he loved to write was bus numbers. So bus timetables, newspapers, stolen documents, hymn books and Bibles were embellished with 'Mr G. W. E. Cochran' in writing. Wilfred Ernest were his dad's names (both of which Will hated). Including Dad's initials in his signature emphasised for Gordon the link between the two men, father and son, both occupied in similar distinguished careers.

Down all the years he has never realised that writing his name on stolen goods is a bad move.

Page numbers in any book that Gordon fancied were viewed as bus numbers, page 44 having an A added to it, thus recording the number of his local bus. The Bible had numbered chapters and psalms, which were enhanced by becoming bus numbers, creating a sort of heavenly time-table. Real, orthodox timetables were a rich source of delight. They were reduced to rags by the intense, dense, writing, editing every page. Such hard work! Indeed, any page with lists or numbers or addresses was edited and modified and enriched. Gordon learned to write his address, more or less, which upgraded his editing skills.

There were so few significant things my brother could do, that when he learned a new skill, it pretty well took him over. Something which he previously could not do, became something he couldn't stop doing. In spite of the consistent efforts of his family and friends and supporters to protect their treasured books and magazines and documents, the day inevitably came when the Enthusiastic Editor struck and delightedly, in his own particular way, left his mark.

Will, loving church music, and wanting to enjoy it on his piano, bought himself a brand-new Church of Ireland Hymnal. Gordon was deeply interested. Sharing his dad's pleasure, and not having mastered the piano himself, he did his best to enhance the Hymnbook. He cared nothing for hymn numbers as hymn numbers, but they were wonderful raw material for him to transform. He transformed them. When this particular work was completed, something he could be proud of, he went happily to tuck the new Special Edition hymnbook into the bookcase.

He couldn't. *It wouldn't fit.* His careless impractical dad hadn't foreseen this problem. Never mind, Gordon thought seriously and creatively. He found the kitchen scissors, and with some difficulty, cut and chopped the hymnbook down to size, and slid it smoothly into its new place of honour.

When our rage died down, and we dried our tears, how could we not love him?

Charmingly, in following his business career, when he was writing Gordon imitated his father's manner. There was a settling into the best position, and a way of 'addressing' the page with a little flourish of the pen, before signing his name. The image of his dad.

5

DUMBFOUNDED

MY brother couldn't talk.

A chubby blundering toddler is adorable; a late-developing four-year-old can cause bedlam.

One day when Gordon was big enough to be physically formidable my cousin Alan came to visit our house. The table had been set for a meal in the dining room, and the food was in place. When Alan arrived, Gordon had just pulled the cloth completely off the table, bringing everything with it, food, china, hot tea, milk... The carpet was covered with an appalling mess. Lydia was weeping.

Things were changing. Gordon was becoming harder to manage, and throwing tantrums that were seriously challenging.

Lydia tried by love and understanding to help the boy to avoid rages. Will tried to reason with him, and to succeed by disciplining him. Lydia was afraid that Will would have a heart attack. Observing our mother and father parenting their boy, we realised again that patience is not something you have, it's something you do. Prayer helped, something else my sister and I saw in action.

My friend Hilary started in Wesley with me when we were nine. When Gordon was born, Hilary's mother visited mine in the nursing home. Afterwards Hilary heard her mother – who had seen Gordon at just a few days old – saying that Lydia would have her hands full in the future, and would need all the support and the prayers that she could get.

When Hilary and I were aged about 15, she visited our house. She remembers feeling afraid of Gordon. She hadn't seen anybody like him before. He was such an odd little fellow, who made strange unintelligible noises, and did unreasonable, unexpected things.

But, one day many years later, Hilary went to see my parents, who were by that time living in Greystones with Gordon. Some time after that visit Hilary wrote to me. A much happier memory!

'I visited your parents in Greystones, and I remember Gordon insisting on walking me back to the bus. We chatted away and he literally handed me over to the conductor (who obviously knew him) in a lovely, old-fashioned, gentlemanly way.'

So, if he couldn't talk, how did Gordon chat with Hilary?

When he was a baby, he made experimental sounds. 'Goggengoggengoggen' was a blurred, smudged sort of noise, singsong. Did it mean anything? Did he know that it could, or should, mean something? A tiny infant doesn't decide or choose to send out a wind-in-tummy alarm call, or a sopping-wet-nappy misery wail, he cries involuntarily. But his brain develops, and after a while, watching people talking and responding, and hearing their speech, he begins to want to communicate, and then words become his tools.

The tools are primitive, they are blunt. Over time, with use they become sharp, and his handling of the tools becomes skilled and precise.

If anyone is to speak rather than only to laugh or cry, he needs to have a thought, however simple. For him to point at a 'thing' and to simply say its name is speech. But to say 'I want that thing' is more complicated.

'Take that thing away, it frightens me!'

'The thing is mine, you can't have it.'

'I'd like to give my thing to somebody else.'

Gordon was growing, sitting up (well, propped up) and looking around at his world. He seemed to want to communicate. Will gave him the benefit of the doubt, and would talk back to him, making use of Gordon's own sound, Goggengoggen. Gordon gradually changed this into a sound like Go'ser, Gobser. We thought the boy was trying to say his own name, surely a hopeful sign? Ultimately he turned it into Gogo, and today that's his name, informally, among family and friends.

Gestures helped Gordon to convey simple messages to us, and he never learned to speak in the sense of putting more than two words together, and the simple words in his vocabulary didn't convey much.

Confounded

Baffled, confused, perplexed, never muddled, not mute, but wordless, muzzled, not dumb, but pent-up, imprisoned.

How impertinent it is that I try to describe Gordon's confounded speech, by choosing to pour words onto the page.

When my children and grandchildren were growing past babyhood, we saw the stages at which Gordon's speech development stopped dead. The following is one example.

Chloe Lydia, our first grandchild, had made up some primitive names for special things she saw around the house. At Christmas the names included a word for decorations, and one to use for a shining string of silver musical notes which was hanging on the wall. The notes were partly hidden round a corner of the room, so a word was found for that hiddenness too. With her very own new skill, using her three words, the little girl made up her first sentence, excitedly squeaking 'Oh! Dec-dec lah-lah peep-oh!' She was sixteen months old. I do seem to remember almost her first proper word was anemometer, but that was because she lived near Dun Laoghaire pier, where there was one. She didn't know it was a hard word, so she said it.

Gordon's speech never went as far as Chloe's three-word

sentence. Although his vocabulary did grow, most of his words were hard to identify. He couldn't make the sound that he needed to make; did he not hear it in his head? Did he know that the sound wasn't right – or did he just think we were all incredibly stupid? He didn't try to clarify or re-shape the word. It was stuck. Dumb.

When Gordon was sixty, our son Jeremy and his wife Susie brought their young children to visit him in Greystones. Florence, aged five, was intrigued. Her little brother, Tillman, aged three, was happy to murmur little remarks to Gordon, and then to implode with happy shyness. Florence watched, thinking. Afterwards there were discussions at home about how Gordon makes his words, and why he's like that. One of Florence's friends has Down Syndrome, and that was discussed too. They all studied the calendar produced by the Down Syndrome Ireland organisation, which I had bought in Avoca Handweavers shop in Suffolk Street.

Speech therapists did their best. The Irish writer Christy Brown, who couldn't speak clearly but who was an intellectual giant, wrote:

> Painting became everything to me... Through it all I made articulate all that I saw and felt, all that went on inside the mind that was housed within my useless body like a prisoner in a cell.

Christy was fully self-aware, and could articulate his experience.

Cogito, ergo sum. I ponder, therefore I exist.

Gordon. He thinks and ponders, he cogitates, we see him doing it, we watch him and wonder. And he abundantly, triumphantly *is*. He exists. That's it. The mysterious man; his secrets are unfathomable. We'll never know him.

He can't speak words of criticism or enquiry. He can't blaspheme, be rude, ask about the past or the future, he can't ask about God, or about Jesus, whom he has been taught to love. He can't understand sinfulness, or redemption.

However, though his speech remained pretty hopeless, he

learned to understand what was said to him while he was still a very young boy.

Understanding speech was good.

Mother says, 'Gogo, we're going out to the shops'. He knows what that means, understands the basic sense of it. Good, an adventure! I like the shops.

And it was bad.

People say things to him that he doesn't want to know. He doesn't want to go to the shops. He's a busy five-year-old playing happily with a toy bus, and going out means stopping what he's doing and getting all togged up, and then the tedium of trailing round after his mother, being held on to. He looks up, and he can't negotiate:

'Mum can I have a few minutes to finish my game?

'Mum I'm too tired to go out.'

'But we went to the shops yesterday.'

'Can I have an ice cream for being good?'

'Do I have to go?'

Emotions are flooding his mind, and he can't say anything.

'You're so mean, always stopping my fun!'

'Why can't I ever do what I want?'

'I hate you!'

Smash! The bus hits the table and knocks over the jug of milk. Gordon is for a moment delighted, but then, reacting in panic he throws himself against a dining chair, and he and the chair crash to the floor. Now furious and terrified, he fetches up next to his mum and lands a kick on her leg.

He's roaring with frustration, and her eyes are swimming with tears.

Yes, I know. Tantrums are common enough with little children, but most children eventually reach the age of reason, and they and their parents learn how to negotiate, to bargain, and best of all, how to talk things over. And my illustration is unfair to Lydia's sensitivity in handling Gordon. However, the best parent can't avoid offending their child sometimes!

Where every word is at home, taking its place to support
the others... The complete consort dancing together.

T.S.Eliot, poet, using his word-gift to tell us how it should be

Gordon began to understand most of what was said to him. He felt a response, and he wanted, strained and fought to say what was in his mind, hidden. But the words would not come.

Speech therapy was no help at all. He hadn't any speech to be fixed.

People talking without speaking.

Paul Simon

Dumbfounded Gordon may have been and confounded, but eventually he became an enthusiastic conversationalist, ingeniously finding ways around the ridiculously dead bits of his brain, and calling on all his strength of character and his creative gifts to enhance his relationship with his family and his friends.

We're great talkers in our family. Gordon needed to talk. T.S. Eliot, the master wordsmith, wrote:

Trying to learn to use words, and every attempt
is a wholly new start, and a different kind of failure.

Will kept researching ways in which his son could be mended. Lydia tried to work with what was already there. Will dreamed of an awakening, a reviving of the ruined speech centre. Alongside his interest in homeopathy, he was intrigued with the possibility of going beyond other familiar boundaries of medicine and therapies. 'Fringe' and 'Alternative' were not derogatory terms in our dad's vocabulary, for anything. To him they meant fresh thinking, discovery, intellectual adventure.

In April, 1961, my dad sat in the window of La Villa Borghèse, à Neuilly, in Paris, and watched his wife walking along the street towards the shops. How scared she was! How brave she was! This was her first time abroad, she spoke no French, and she was all alone in the street among strangers.

Lydia wrote:

> Never forget on the train to Paris, full of fears, I re-discovered this verse. 'In the same way, the Spirit helps us in our weakness. We do not know what we ought to pray for, but the Spirit himself intercedes for us with groans that words cannot express... the Spirit intercedes for the saints in accordance with God's will.' *Romans 8:26*

Her husband turned around and smiled at the little boy snuggled on the bed behind him. 'Well, Gogo, mummy has gone out all by herself! She'll be back soon, and she'll tell us all about it.'

This was one of two odysseys to a clinic in Paris. My parents had been in consultations with a Dublin doctor, and believed that the treatment at this place offered hope. The doctors in Paris specialised in the injection of cells. As far as I understood, these cells, whose provenance I never knew, were meant to kick-start the damaged bits of Gordon's brain into life. Or perhaps to stimulate quiescent cells into action, expecting that they would migrate to the area of the brain where they were needed. Years later, I have wondered if this was a precursor of today's stem cell treatment. My question is, if so, where did the cells come from? And did that experimental procedure ever have success?

Royal Jelly was also used therapeutically, I think. Fortunately I'm not attempting to write a Medical Treatise on Spectacular Ways to Regenerate the Disfunctional Brain. It's just the Story of Gordon.

For the first visit Lydia accompanied Will and Gordon, and they parked Dorothy and me with friends. My clearest, and slightly horrid, memory of that kind hospitality was of a laburnum tree abundantly spilling its golden blossom over the gateway, the drooping blooms complete with tiny wormy things hanging on gossamer. I tried, desperately, to dodge them.

On the other occasion when I was parked, it was with my Uncle Sam and Auntie Mabel Cochran up on the Hill of Howth. From that happy interlude I took away The Story of San Michele by Axel Munthe, which I had fallen in love with. More precisely, I stole it.

The second time, Will and Gordon went together for more injections, a boys' adventure. Will wrote to me, letters full of love for his little boy, and pride at his courage.

Nobody had promised that the treatments would be effective. Though worth trying, they were just shots in the dark.

When all Else Fails ...from the troubles
of the world I turn to newspapers.

(With apologies to F.W Harvey)

Gordon's mother, knowing her boy intimately, started to show him things in The Irish Times, pointing out the words. She taught him to recognise place names which he was already used to hearing in conversation. He was shown the names of people he knew, which sometimes appeared as preachers in the Church Notices for the following Sunday. Occasionally they found gold in the Births, Deaths and Marriages columns.

Music was in the pages. Orchestral concert announcements, radio programmes, were lovely. He studied them, knowing that they were his thing.

This doesn't sound very significant, being a way for Lydia to entertain her son rather than to impart skill. In fact it was the best possible teaching, clearly inspired. Together Gordon and his mother explored the riches of his adored newspaper, together. His Irish Times, the paper of record, just for him.

Gordon learned to recognise days of the week, and dates. As well as immersing themselves in the Irish Times, the two partners diversified into studying bus timetables, which Gordon already loved (and edited mercilessly), and he learned to recognise the names of places where friends lived, and the buses that served those places.

With the enriching of his life, he learned to recognise news of strikes, bombs, crashes. And he loved photos of beautiful women wearing evening gowns, with very high heels. He would suggest hopefully that certain young women whom he liked might dress like that. And he would chuckle.

So, when Gordon wanted to impart a nugget of news, to talk about somebody whose name he couldn't say, he would turn up the number of the bus which served this friend's home, and stab a finger at it. Lydia would churn her brains – 'Who gets the 51A...? Oh yes! It's Eddie and Greta!' So she would make a conversation about these church friends, and Gordon would beam, his face pink with pleasure. He had had a chat with his mum.

Gordon chatted mostly with his mother. Often she couldn't understand what he was bursting to tell her, and it became a race for her to work out what he meant, or to make an inspired guess, before he lost patience. The newspaper and timetable skills didn't always provide a clue.

From toddlerhood, when he was enraged, Gordon used physical force, and for many years, while he was growing up, that continued. So he hit his mother, thumped her, shoved her. She cried, not only from physical pain, but heartbroken that her son had buffeted her. Afterwards he held out his hand to her in forgiveness, possibly even in repentance.

With maturity he learned patience. He would stand, with a bit of news, rummaging through his brain to come up with some clue that would break the deadlock. You could hear him thinking. He would remember a reference to some link; a different bus number, a demonstration of what that person was known to do; maybe he cycled to work, or there might be a dog in the picture – 'Wuff Wuff'. Gordon used 'Dog!' as a term of derision at the antics of some wayward hound.

A friend had a car crash; this made him distinctive, a gift for Gordon. Theatrically indicating a car crash – instead of just learning the blessed man's name! – was a nice touch in a conversation. My brother was impressed by the drama of car crashes.

Years later Gordon and his parents were involved in a crash, none of them being injured, but the ride in an ambulance was a rich experience.

In fact, apart from learning to read – in his very limited way – my brother's intellectual strengths proved to be a stupendously retentive memory, and a forensic skill in cutting linguistic Gordian knots.

6

MY SISTER, AND ME

WE had lives too. I kept a diary. Dorothy didn't, but if she had, what would she have confided to it?

That she was lonely. That she dearly loved her sweet, aimless little brother. That she hadn't enough friends. That her teachers were mean, or kind, disapproving, fair or not fair, that they gave her too much homework, they didn't believe her when she explained why it wasn't done; they were cruel, sent out bad reports just for spite, sent sneaky notes to her parents, they had it in for her, and sometimes, they were really, really nice to her.

She might record in her diary that her family simply couldn't understand her, and she couldn't make head or tail of them. Visitors to our home might have had a place in Dorothy's diary pages. Would she write about the kindness of our parents' friends, the love they showered her with, the little gifts, the comfort of being settled on an uncle's lap, the jokes and the simple lighthearted fun?

In her diary she might have recorded that looking in the mirror was a pleasure; she was very pretty, and she didn't look at all like any of us. Her hair was copper-gold, her eyes were the blue of the sky, and her fair skin was pink and white like blossom. She had the loveliest, happiest, most radiant smile.

My name would have appeared in the diary. How we played, how we fought, wanting to kill each other, how I teased her and put her down, how I made clothes for her, gave her presents, how I took her to town and lost her in Henry Street.

The names of friends would have appeared in Dorothy's diary, Joyce at the top of the road, a friend from school. Another friend who lived across the road. Boys' names might have dotted the pages, boys whom we never knew.

Her diary would have told us that she left Wesley before doing Inter (Junior) Cert exam, and how not fair it was that she was victimised; how after that she worked in a bookshop, but not for long.

Dorothy would have described how proud she was to start training in the Children's Sunshine Home. Nobody else in the family was qualified in childcare. She learned to say and to spell phenylketonuria. When she was requested to leave the Sunshine Home, she realised that she hated it anyway.

She was pretty nearly grown-up by this time.

The Diarist

I started to write my diary in 1957, when I was fifteen. At that time, Dorothy was twelve, and Gordon was three.

My diary wasn't like my mother's, written in the margins of Streams in the Desert, seeking after God, and drawing strength and comfort from Him. It was where I jotted down the utterly absorbing trivia of my teenage life. What follows is what I wrote, the truth, verbatim though incomplete. I left out a bit here and there.

> 1957. Gordon's still coughing badly, a fire in his room all day, mum with him to keep him warm and resting. Dad sleeping with him, me with mum.
>
> He fell in Duffy's, nose bled. I'm making a frock for Dorothy.
>
> Dreaming about the current boy interest.
>
> Trying to work for Inter Cert.
>
> Mum weak and fainty from G's illness, dad in Cork for 3 days. I stayed home from school. Dorothy's a demon.

Some of Gordon's favourite things. Drawing by Abigail Chipperfield Smith.

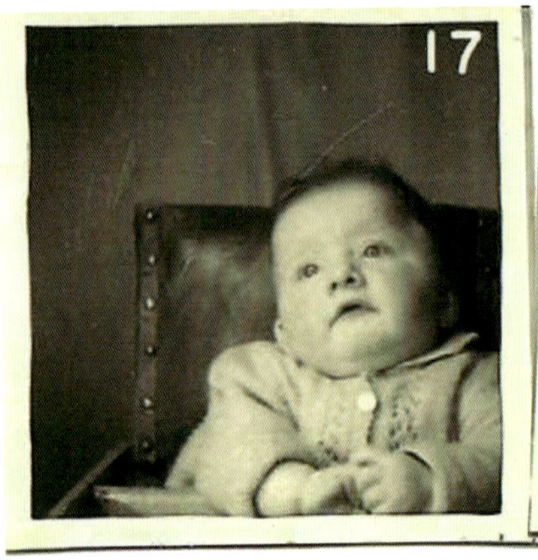

Gordon, little dreamy fellow.

With Ruth and Dorothy.

The bus conductor.

Family group
about 1957.

At Keith and Ruth's wedding, 1964, aged 10

Dorothy, Ruth and Lydia with Gordon (above); and on Greystones beach with sister Dorothy, about 1960 (right).

In school, aged 10.

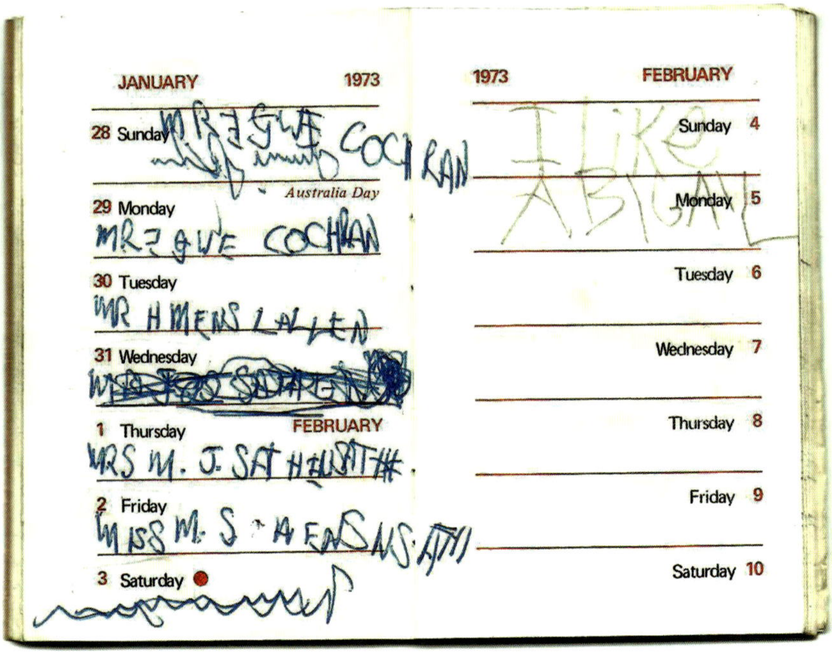

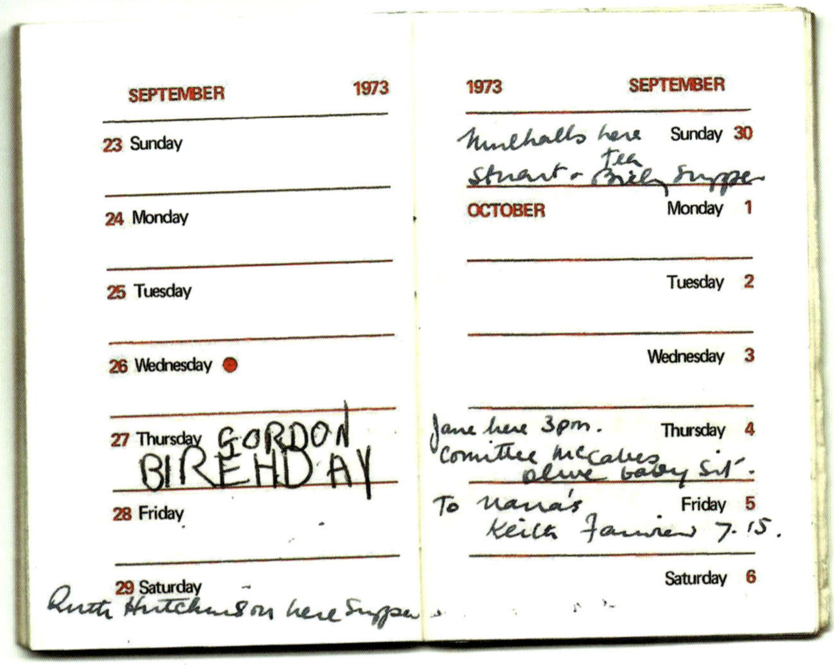

Gordon writes in Ruth's diary, including his friend's names (top), and his birthday (above), in 1973.

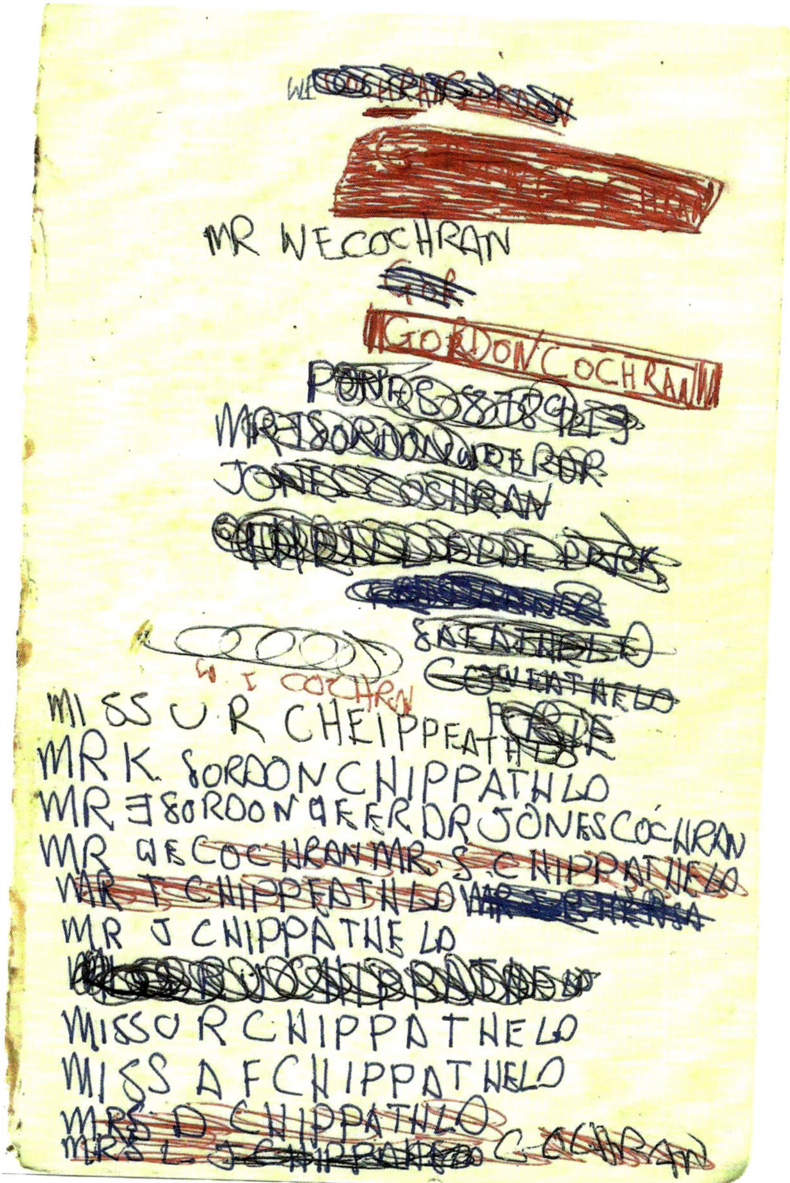

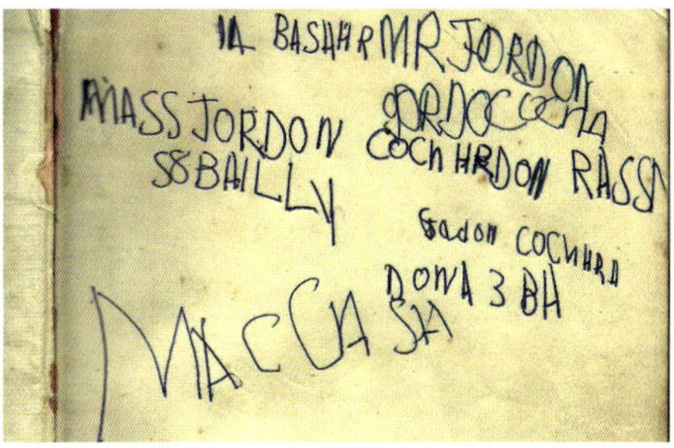

Handel's *Messiah*, flyleaf (above); and Mendelssohn's *Elijah* (right).

Making sense of the Special Olympics, 1985.

Was called to Principal's office. Dad wrote about my lateness. Was excused – G. the reason of course.

Finished Dor's frock – beautiful.

Life's drab, not allowed to go to rugby international with a boy unless others come too. Mum so tired.

Having the time of my life, juggling boys.

Went to youth group, he wasn't there.

Went to match with him, his cousin Keith was there.

Such fun, messages relayed, phone calls waiting for, joy of meeting, gloom at being let down.

Life's not really happy. School friend often absent.

Found Dorothy sobbing her heart out over a book in which a boy was dying. Sentimental little...

I shot my first goal, for 2nd XI. A senior boy asked who I was. Oh, bliss!

Everybody lets you down. School friends nasty, I kept my dignity, such as it was.

Love again!

Tore his letter in half.

Dor's birthday. She's so bad and so sweet.

April 10. The Day Centre for the Association of Parents and Friends of Mentally Handicapped Children was opened by Mrs Seán T. O'Kelly.

Dad & I stood on the landing till 11 pm, talking about atoms, humanity, gases etc.

(Loads of bad colds, having hard times. Hilary so often absent.)

Inter Cert.

Mum fell, Gogo bumped his head, in bed together, mum very shaken.

1958. Jan 12. Awful report. Dad well, mother sick, very bad cold, desperate cough. By lunchtime I was sick, shivering, weeping all the time. My temp higher than mum's!

Dad stayed home. Aunt came round.

Everybody's dying, people dear to us.

Another one died. Dorothy stayed home to help. Bless the child.

Difficult day, mum gets mad at Dor. I wish and ache to go away somewhere.

A much better day, Gogo sweet and co-operative, Dorothy good, mum and I better, things more peaceful.

Dad has a cold, Doreen wears lipstick, I'm in a vile temper, Mum gave out reams – I'm lazy, not working etc etc. Things are depressing enough without lectures.

I stayed home to help, baked cakes and tarts and sausage rolls, missed a symphony concert on the radio, and cried. Gogo a sweet debonair pal.

Between boyfriends. So depressed.

Savage day. Beastly house. Total of 8 children visiting, plus neighbours, big dog Jock, Bundle, and Gordon. All squabbling.

Classroom overlooking Children's Hospital, waving to a sweet little boy, who waved back frantically.

I read 'I Leap over the Wall', Monica Baldwin.

A young man from dad's office delivering documents, asked me to a dance! Embarrassed to have to say No Thanks.

Dorothy is impossible. A demon. Bless her. She's so lovely, she's growing up quickly, and vividly pretty. An angel all day.

How I love books. 'Yankee Stranger', by Elswyth Thane.

Blue suit!!! 8½ guineas. Hat!

To London with Dad. Can't bear the thought of leaving Gordon and mum. He's so dear and clinging.

Cosy cabin on the boat. Convinced thumb kept me from feeling sick.

Dec 25. Gordon very good, overwhelmed by new train, bike and bus. I finally shook off a 'perfectly nice boy' who had pursued me for a couple of years, and fell headlong in love (temporarily) with another one.

1959. June 17. Finished school!!!! Discovered that the romantic dreamboat was too charming and too argumentative.

December. Carol Party. Partnered Keith Chipperfield.

Jan 16 1960. Coffee with Keith.

Throughout these years, Lydia went regularly to prayer-meetings held in Bethany Home, from which Dorothy had been adopted. The Home had been administered and managed by people who were Evangelical Christians, it was a Protestant Home. Money was always short, because for various reasons the charity wasn't considered to be eligible for financial support from the State or from the established churches. In the 1940s, when Dorothy was there, few if any of the staff had spent years training in childcare, or studying child psychology, or investigating special diets, or striving to develop the flowering of each child's unique personality. Getting some food on the table, keeping the babies and toddlers warm and safe and loved, with clean clothes and a clean environment, and with the luxury of a few toys, was the challenging business of every day.

February 1962. My two best friends, Hilary and Daphne came to tea. I made it. Feminine chat is lovely.

Keith preached. Delicious.

I love him more every day.

I played mixed hockey for the company, studied NT Greek, learned the violin, sang in choirs.

I left K to the Dun Laoghaire boat. Cried when I left him. He nearly cried in his cabin. Shucks!

K slept here overnight, I slept with Dor. Funny to see him in my bed in the morning, tousled & sleepy-eyed. Gordon dived in beside him, a little bare-naked boy.

April. Mummy has German Measles.

Gordon has German measles, mild convulsions – high temp. Mum dead tired.

Sept 1. Engaged to Keith. So happy. Big party at home.

1964. Dorothy wants to become a Catholic and marry Jim D.

May 9. We married.

Our wedding photos show Gordon, 10 years old, with a fresh haircut, wearing a short-trousered suit, spick-and-span shirt and tie, and in his buttonhole a Flower. This was the beginning of a life-long passion for big buttonhole flowers. He's never been inspired by rosebuds. Never mind suits and ties (although he did become very attracted to ties – other people's ties), a good big blossom occupying the vacant lapel gave a man a certain finish. And you never knew when a wedding might suddenly take place.

We pondered whether Gogo's passion for a floral buttonhole was a genetic quirk. Gordon wasn't the first in the family with the quirk! A relative from my parents' generation had roamed through Dublin, dropping in to hotels here and there. If there happened to be a wedding, he would mingle happily, prepared, because he was rarely without a blooming flower on his lapel. He could, and often did, sing. One day I sat with him on the front seat in a bus, and I was shrinking with embarrassment as he sang some ditty. Today if that happened, I'd be thrilled! Delightfully, and criminally, this gent would pick a handy flower out of any garden he sauntered past. I don't think he actually trespassed, but a rose growing beside the gate, a dahlia or a chrysanthemum, a sprig of prunus within reach – the temptation to pilfer a pretty thing was irresistible.

The buttonhole habit had its most spectacular flowering much later, when my brother was almost sixty. His favoured bloom for a whole season was a green hydrangea, nearly as big as his face, a stunner, snipped each day from the bush in the garden, and pinned onto his overburdened, wilting lapel.

Umbrellas

15B Isaac's for lunch

Salome

KELLY

Clontarf Bus Garage

Springer the dog

Peter

POSY THE DOG

Paris

Footprints for lunch

HELLO!

Carols in St Patrick's

SCRIPTURE UNION CAMPS

Connolly Station

7

NOT ALONE

Screw your courage to the sticking place, and we'll not fail.

Shakespeare, Macbeth

'Association for Parents of Mentally Backward Children.
Lady wishing to form above
wishes to contact anyone interested.'

ON Thursday 2nd June 1955 this notice was placed in The Irish Times by Patricia Farrell, whose son Brian had Down Syndrome. Mrs Farrell was shocked to find that there were no school options for him. The only service available at that time for people with an intellectual disability was institutional residential care.

This modest message resulted in a public meeting being held in Dublin's Mansion house, following which St Michael's House was founded.

The organisation's first Medical Director was Dr Barbara Stokes. She said, 'We rushed in where many would fear to venture. The one essential was to meet and help parents who came to us, not so much for a diagnosis, as for advice about what they should or could do to help their child with a disability'.

The first service St Michael's House set up was a small day school – for people who quite possibly, indeed probably, could never learn anything that the rest of society would value. In itself it was a startling innovation. As the organisation followed that by establishing residential and day centres, its central belief became clearer and more compelling – that people with intellectual disabilities are full and equal members of society.

The Founders of St Michael's House had great courage, and they did not fail.

It was recorded in 2011 that the organisation provided services for 1,585 children and adults with intellectual disabilities, and their families, across the Greater Dublin area.

Lydia was inspired by the initiative, and with the support of Doris Hodgins, her friend, she attended the early meetings of St Michael's House, and subsequent lectures on the management of these 'problem' children. Heartbreaking stories were told of mothers at the end of their strength, coping with a large family which included what would now be called a Special Needs child, in tiny overcrowded homes. Compared with these, Gordon didn't seem to be particularly troublesome.

Dr Stokes was especially warm towards Lydia, and she was very helpful in discussing Gordon's problems, and in advising and encouraging their management.

I find it poignant that Lydia's chief support came from her friend Doris, who had two children the same age as Gordon. Two! Boy and girl twins who were perfectly healthy and intellectually bright, as well as an older son who was a mother's dream. That quiver-full of children was in sharp contrast with my mother's armful. The two women, different in circumstance and in temperament, were committed to living lives that honoured God.

So, Doris was unfalteringly generous with her friendship and with her time and her energy. These were matchless gifts to Lydia. Lydia was upheld by Doris's steadiness, and she got her courage from God. In the Bible, in the book written by Micah, there's a question and an answer:

'What does the Lord require of you?
'To act justly and to love mercy and
to walk humbly with your God.'

Doris and Lydia both walked like this. In my mum's case, I know, because I saw it. I know that the walk was difficult.

'I am the Lord your God, who takes hold of your right hand and says to you, Do not fear; I will help you'.

When Lydia stumbled, she didn't try hoisting herself up by her bootstrings. She felt the hand of God holding hers. She walked on with him, her soul steady and strong.

St Michael's House opened their first Day Centre in Finglas, North Dublin.

What is this that roareth thus? Can it be a Motor Bus? Yes, the smell and hideous hum, Indicat Motorem Bum!

A.D.Godley

Early one morning, it was with a very shining morning face that Gordon, all dressed up, hanky in pocket, glasses polished, stepped out with his mother. Shakespeare would have been astonished – this schoolboy didn't whine, or gloomily creep like a snail! He and his mum stepped out with high courage. They took the 44A bus to Marino, crossed the busy main road, and waited at the stop for the bus to Finglas.

Two buses to go to school! Two buses to go home! Is there any better way to spend the day? The buses had a wonderful smell, and a glorious hum. It was a bit less glorious for Gordon's mother, but that's what she did, over and over again, till Gordon learned to do it himself.

A journey to work or to school without your mother is much more fun than with her. Men didn't get on and off wonderful smelly humming buses encumbered with a mother! Gordon grew in wisdom and in street-smartness and in favour with buses and conductors and drivers and inspectors, and he enjoyed meeting a rich variety of fellow travellers.

I don't know when he became friendly with the proprietor of Mac's shoe repair shop in Marino, but that shop was a punctuation point in Gordon's early travels. He met with great kindness.

Neither do I know what he learned in school. Going to Finglas, and I think, later to Ballymun, kept him out of mischief! As well as possibly learning the odd snippet of 'school' stuff, he grew to be a most gracious, kind man. Lydia, who still couldn't help making friends, got to know the regulars who bussed their way to school, then later, to workshop. She knew their names, and chatted with them - or to them. Good fellowship and warm delighted smiles were enough, and Gordon observed these lovely sociable exchanges. As he matured, he made these skills his own.

The Right Hand of Fellowship

When you call on a friend unexpectedly, he opens the door and greets you with pleasure. His impulse is to shake hands. Then, 'Oh, give me a minute, I've been weeding/cleaning the oven/painting the piano/kneading bread, I need to wash my hands'. You wait, and a minute later your friend comes back and extends to you his damp clean hand. If you're the hugging type (who isn't, these days?), you wrap each other in a Bear Hug. Because you are Friends.

What we do know is that every spare space in Gordon's brain seems to be stuffed with Friends.

Apart from family and neighbours, and people in school or sheltered workshop, many of Gordon's friends came from among the people who attended his church. That was initially Fairview Hall, and later, in Greystones, it was both the churches that he believed he belonged to. In a church environment he had no inhibitions or sense of shyness, so he took ownership, in the most charming way. If there was welcoming to be done, he did it. He was pretty fussy about time-keeping, so he was likely to greet the last few people to arrive anywhere, with ''ate!' stabbing at his watch. The word was self-explanatory!

The church services normally included three or 4 hymns, some prayer, a Bible reading, and a sermon, or preaching. It was more usually referred to as 'speaking'. Since we had no ordained ministers, the teaching was done by ordinary men from our church, or by visiting speakers. They generally had full-time jobs, and in their private lives they were Bible scholars. Their ministry was spiritual and practical.

When this type of church activity is done without ritual or a prescribed liturgy a preacher can forget to keep an eye on the time. No matter, Gordon would rise to the occasion, and helpfully point to his watch. If the unfortunate speaker in Fairview Hall, absorbed in passing on what he had learned from Scripture, didn't notice the interruption, my peerless brother stood up and, anxious only to help, told him to Stop. Those episodes didn't initially make a new friend for him, but he would be so charming afterwards, such an artlessly chummy little man, that no preacher could stand on his dignity. Like it or not, he became a friend.

The large city centre church, Merrion Hall (now The Davenport Hotel, close to Merrion Square), was another one like ours, only very much bigger. In Gordon-speak, it was 'hooge'. A Missionary Conference took place there annually, and large numbers of people came to it from across the country and from Northern Ireland, even from the UK. It was a Foretaste of Heaven for Gordon. Moving through the aisles to find a seat; going downstairs to the lower ground floor where hundreds of people met for tea at long tables, eating sandwiches filled with minced ham; standing with mum and dad on a balcony with the hooge crowd all round him singing hymns, was joy unconfined. And each one of these people had a hand which Gordon wanted to shake.

The chairman and eminent speakers occupied a sort of extended podium in the middle of the church auditorium. They too had eminently shakeable hands. Gordon easily overcame the challenge of their physical elevation. After the meeting ended, he confidently wended his way around behind the platform and up the steps, and he was able to greet the startled gentlemen with his trustful outstretched hand.

Instead of a normal speaker at our own church, we occasionally had a visit from The Dublin Male Voice Choir. During the service they sang several times, in harmony, making the loveliest sound, and then one of the members would teach from the Bible. We in Gordon's family and in his close circle knew that when he was excited, my brother would mutter, squeak, chuckle, laugh out loud, and generally enter into the spirit of the occasion. We were quite used to that, and comfortable with his forms of expression. When the DMVC visited us, from the first moment he was excited. The commotion which the choir members began to hear, from the back of the congregation, was made by the happiest, most thrilled little boy. It was a matchless, unique tribute to them.

Gordon didn't know, none of us knew at the time, that one of the bass singers in the choir would become his brother-in-law, my husband, the kindest, funniest, most patient brother a Gordon-boy could possibly have.

Church situations offered unexpected pleasures. Many years later he was in a meeting in Greystones where the building was very near to a railway line. The track was raised on an embankment. The meeting was under way, when Gordon became possessed! Up he stood, and with grand gestures and loud voice he announced that a train was coming. It roared and rumbled by, and not a soul on that train knew that, stunning audience and speaker alike, an enraptured little man was nearly exploding with joy.

In the 1960s David Wilson, a student attending Trinity College, became a friend of my family. On one visit, he responded to our request that he would play the piano for us. Gordon was delighted, and he nearly wept with excitement when, at a particularly demanding point, David crossed his hands. What a thing to do! Ruth never did it. Dad couldn't do it. David Wilson, international missionary, distinguished Director of a mission organisation, and no mean pianist, was thereafter signed by Gordon Cochran as the Man with the Crossed Hands.

When they met at a DART station forty years later, Gordon knew his old friend, and confirmed it by making the Sign of the Crossed Hands. David tells us that during the subsequent journey 'Gordon, in all innocence, expressed his warmth toward my wife Pam by placing his hand on Pam's knee. What did the passengers think? We didn't care.'

My parents were very hospitable. People always came round on Sunday nights. Gordon enjoyed this, he loved having visitors. But unfortunately, not for long. When he felt it was time for them to go home, even if they'd arrived thirty minutes ago, he would gather up their coats, and distribute them round, imparting his sense of urgency that they should go back to their own places, and leave us in peace.

'The time has come,' the Walrus said, 'to talk of many things'.

For some reason, Gordon's word for a train was, indeed is, Bum-Bum. There must have been a reason, as there has been for every one of his words. His own invention, probably based on the sound of the mainline diesel locomotive-hauled trains which he adored. Big brutes, beloved by our boy.

If Gordon's life were a tapestry, the pattern would be stitched by trains! Albert Stuart wrote to me of seeing him in Pearse Railway Station in Dublin. Al was waiting for the northbound commuter train to Rush, while Gordon walked up and down the opposite platform, waiting for the DART to Greystones.

> 'He was always so dapper with his rolled brolly hanging from one arm, under which was tucked his copy of The Financial Times, while in the other hand he held his briefcase. He was well known to the station personnel, and would wave in his inimitable fashion whenever

one of them came along. It was remarkable to observe how they looked out for him to make sure he got onto the correct train, especially if there had been an alteration to their schedule.

It used to amuse me to see how the train drivers would spot Gordon and respond with a loud beep on their horn as Gordon would swing his arm up to check the time of arrival against his wrist watch.

Whenever I came close enough to him to say hello, he never failed to extend his hand for a very firm handshake. May he continue to have years of health and happiness to enjoy his own space, wherever that may be.'

I had my own Gordon experience, which started at Pearse Station. After he had moved to live in Greystones, he and I used to meet in town sometimes for lunch. He spent most of his time adventuring, and he needed to eat. He couldn't manage an ordinary restaurant, being unable to say what he wanted, and he wouldn't have been quite reliable about paying. An arrangement had been made with the management of the restaurant attached to the Isaacs Hostel in Frenchman's Lane. The staff had agreed to give him lunch each day, and to bill his carers monthly. They were immensely kind, learning what he liked to eat, and giving him extra treats. When he said it was his birthday – the Birthday Song was unmistakable – 'La-la Lah Lah hyoo-hoo... me!' they brought out a little cake, with candles. They probably made a loss on his patronage.

The only thing the staff particularly asked him to do was to come for lunch before 12.30, when the place would begin to fill up with business people. They fascinated him, wasn't he one of them? But somehow they didn't see him as a fellow-toiler; he watched them closely, ready to respond to the hand of business-fellowship. It was rarely, if ever, extended to him.

The real problem for the Isaac's staff was that when Gordon sat down at a table, he made himself very much at home. For a little man, he has always taken up far too much room. So the briefcase would go onto the chair beside him and the newspapers would be placed on the table, leaving plenty of space in front of him for his meal. He liked to pull his seat out, a bit sideways, so that he could easily view the room, and his legs would be *all over the place.* The most sprawling legs I've ever known. Thus he took up a whole table, which represented money to the proprietors, and therefore they asked him to come in early, before the thrilling luncheon rush.

Several times I've met Gordon at the National Concert Hall for a Tuesday lunchtime concert. He had always been good at turning up to meet people at different familiar places in the city. He was moderately good at being on time. But he was beginning to let people down. He was growing older, and getting a bit casual about time-keeping. So, on one unforgettable Tuesday, 14th April 2009, he and I were to meet to go to a concert at the NCH. I arranged with his carer to put him on a DART train in Greystones, to tell him to get off at Pearse Station, and then to text me to tell me to expect him. It was such a good plan.

I went to Pearse, I got the text from Denise and I waited. When Gordon didn't get off the train he had been put onto, I thought deeply. I crossed over to where there were some station staff members. They all knew Gordon; at this stage in his life it seemed as if all Dublin knew him. But they hadn't seen him that morning. 'He may have gone on to Connolly' they suggested. They sent me back to where I had been, instructing me to hop onto the next train to Connolly Station. I hopped. A free ride!

He wasn't at Connolly, and nobody on the platforms had seen him that day. I went to the office, where there were several useful-looking men. They hadn't seen Gordon. We all thought deeply. One charming man asked me did I know the place where Gordon got his lunch. I did. He offered to take me there, so off we trotted together. Isaacs hadn't seen him either. So I gave up. I had been saying very clearly to everybody I spoke to, that if my brother appeared, they were to tell him I was NOT going to meet him that day. Not then. (Not ever! I added to myself.)

I stood in the street. I had tried everywhere. I was free! I could go shopping! But my unruly conscience smote me. I hopped (again), this time onto a cross-town bus. I got off in Earlsfort Terrace, just in time to see Gordon swaggering in through the Concert Hall gates.

Afterwards he wouldn't say where he wanted to go next (he had told me when I caught up with him that he had needed to go to Howth before meeting me). I wanted to cross the city to Eason's in O'Connell Street, to buy Keith's Railway magazines, and prowl the shops. However, when an enticing bus came along which would have served me well, Gordon went for it. Nothing would have persuaded me to go with him. A very little of him goes a very long way, and I was out of sympathy with him. I walked through Stephen's Green in the sunshine and I was happy.

I wrote to the Iarnród Éireann Customer Relations Officers at Pearse and Connolly stations, telling them the story, and thanking everybody who had helped me. The staff had seemed more concerned for Gordon than I was! I thanked them for the daily kindnesses shown to him. I told them that people pray for Gordon, and that they are part of the answer to those prayers.

On hearing the story, my daughter Virginia suggested that in years to come there could be quasi-Joycean walking tours: Routes Gordon Took and Places He Went.

Except that we rarely knew where he went, and he hadn't got intelligible words for most places. One of his place-names, most elegant in its derivation, came about like this. With his parents he was travelling in Northern Ireland, and a signpost indicated the village of Ahoghill, near Ballymena. His dad loved idiosyncratic bits of information, so he read out this lovely word to Gordon. Gordon had been learning about 'Belfast', where his uncle lived, but

Belfast isn't much of a word. Not beside Ahoghill! So 'Aho' became the name of the capital city of Northern Ireland.

Why is Dublin city called Mye-mye? Anybody's guess. Lah-lah is church, because we sing there. There's no word for preaching, I don't think Gogo takes much notice of preaching, unless it goes on too long. On the other hand 'Lalo' is the toilet – the loo. Maybe there's a connection there. 'Hooge' isn't only applied to crowds. Gordon has great respect for tall men. Well, he's pretty short, so it's easy to impress him. Two highly respected hooge men are Mike, who was one of Gogo's carers, and Ronan Scanlan, a friend of ours whom Gogo warmly looks up to.

8

DO THIS IN MEMORY

ON Sundays in our church at Fairview, in north Dublin, the first morning service, before the second, the 'preaching' one, was what we called the Breaking of Bread. This was Holy Communion, in its simplest form. Everybody who was there, who was a follower of Jesus, was invited to join in by eating a little piece of bread and drinking a sip of wine.

This practice was based on the Bible account of the Last Supper that Jesus ate with his disciples, before He was crucified. He asked them to continue to have this meal, a simple one in which the basic ingredients would have been bread and wine, in His memory, until He comes again for His church. The bread would remind them of His broken body, the wine would represent His blood. Easily understood symbols, representing the most awesome universe-shaking event.

These followers of Jesus, called Christians, were, and are, people who have asked God for forgiveness, because of Jesus's death for them, and because of his resurrection. The sharing of bread and wine is a celebration. Gordon witnessed this each week, and naturally assumed that he would share whatever his family and friends were doing. He saw, without understanding the reasons for it, that it was both serious and happy. He wanted to be fully part of it.

A quandary arose. Boys and girls generally weren't expected to share bread and wine till they were old enough to understand the story of the Gospel, and to choose to follow Jesus. That wasn't a rule – we didn't have rules. It was more a question of being guided by what the Bible said. Communion wasn't an empty rite of passage, it was a personal response. So, there was no rule about an absolute age limit, either upper or lower.

My mother began to speculate that, since he couldn't fully understand communion, Gordon might not be eligible to join in; he certainly hadn't been invited to. The leaders of the church – that is our local church, not The Church Universal – hadn't had this issue to consider before, so when Gordon's parents raised it there was a lot of prayer and of reading relevant parts of the Bible. In the end the decision was made, perfectly and simply. Gordon did what Jesus had asked him to do.

A problem: Gordon has the brain development of a tiny child... but Jesus said,

'Let the little children come to me, and do not hinder them, for the kingdom of heaven belongs to such as these'.

Another problem: Gordon can't do theological discussions. He'll never understand the Gospel, fully... but Jesus said,

'I tell you the truth, unless you change and become like little children, you will never enter the kingdom of heaven'.

A third problem: Gordon can't pray proper prayers, or ask for forgiveness, it's too abstract. When he has hurt his mother, he offers to shake hands. His mind can't see Jesus... but Jesus said,

'Whoever comes to me I will never drive away'.

Matthew 19:14, Matthew 18:3, John 6:37

Well, every word in the Bible is there for a purpose, for our instruction, our comfort, our joy, our reproof, our morality, our relationships, our work ethic, our delight in creation, our eternal salvation, our earthly peace. Could God have overlooked the Gordons of this world? Of course not. Gordon is covered by many more writings than those I've quoted above.

My kid brother had learned, up to the full of his understanding, from his mother and father, that Jesus loved him. Her singing to him when he was little had, while he was yet unaware, filled his heart with the knowledge of God. He started to take bread and wine, in full and glorious fellowship.

While on this question of limited understanding, I remember visiting a very elderly friend in Portrush, in Co Antrim. He had had a long life as a missionary, travelling the world. His wife, a brilliant and Godly woman, was deep in dementia. Ernest Lloyd and I talked about dementia. His beloved Jessie couldn't hold a conversation with him, she couldn't ask a question, or answer one.

Where was she?

In spiritual terms, how can a person who has an intellectual disability be taught about God's love, in a way that gets past that dense curtain, and means something to them?

The Bible has the answer to that:

> He (God) has put his Spirit in our hearts... The Spirit helps us in our weakness... He (God) who searches our hearts knows the mind of the Spirit, because the Spirit intercedes.
> God is revealed to us by His Spirit.
>
> **2 Corinthians 1:22, Romans 8:26, 1 Corinthians 2:10**

God's Holy Spirit can speak to the infant, to the person with brain-injury, to the one who is demented, with perfect clarity according to their need.

So, that was Gordon sorted.

I don't mean that trivially. Answers to the questions were found in God's Word, and that was enough. Will and Lydia had peace in the deepest parts of their minds, and their spirits were at rest.

O come, let us sing unto the Lord; let us make a joyful noise...

Psalm 95

In Gordon we saw some of this 'knowing without understanding'. When he used to stay with me and Keith, and later to live with us, he came to our church on Sunday mornings. He knew many of the people. Billy and his mummymummy Mary and daddydaddy Bill, hooge man Ronan, Charlie, and his wife Dot. Charlie was Gordon's chum, the man's man. Izzy (Isabel) was like an extra sister. Gordon sat with his friends, never with us. He knew the hymns and his voice would swell and subside. He could usually find the number in the hymnbook.

There would be a point in the service when people in the congregation might read from the Bible or pray, or choose a hymn to be sung. Sometimes a theme would develop. Gordon would become busy, consulting the hymnbook, and then he would nudge his neighbour and point to the hymn of his choice. The neighbour would speak up, saying, 'Gordon has asked us to sing number 708,

To God be the Glory! Great things He has done.

One morning when he asked us to sing,

I stand amazed in the presence of Jesus the Nazarene,
and wonder how he could love me...

we smiled delightedly to each other. Gordon had hit the nail on the head. One of the hymns had a line,

'Twill be my joy through the ages to sing of His love for me.

Gordon will sing, fully in tune, and the words will be crystal clear.

My brother's joyful noises have been heard in the most improbable places. He came with us to a Church weekend in

Tramore. On the way there we broke the journey at Mullinavat, in County Kilkenny. Keith and Gordon went into a pub to visit the toilet. Then, the spellbound people in the pub heard Gordon's version of *Onward, Christian Soldiers, marching as to war* pouring out from the Gents loo, gradually seeping into every corner of the building. When the recital was done, Gordon, much relieved and very happy, strode out, saluted everybody in sight and came back to the car.

Keith, brave soul, didn't try to disown his brother-in-law; I think he enjoyed the fun.

Gordon nearly always sang in the loo; hymns of course. Those were what he knew.

> Blest be the tie that binds our hearts in Christian love.
>
> **J. Fawcett**

Every man who has sat beside Gordon in church has suffered from the blessing of the tie. Gogo learned to do a fine knot, but the aligning of the two ends took more skill that he could call on. When a natty dresser comes to doing up the tie, as many of you will know, the success of the operation is judged by the alignment of the tails. If it doesn't work the first time, it's yanked off and done again.

That's wearisome, and it delays someone who needs to go out and get on the road. Gordon surveys himself in the mirror, he picks up the ends of his tie, and he sighs at what he sees. But there's always hope, and inspiration strikes. Off he goes to the kitchen – how could he have forgotten the scissors, his ally in so many dilemmas? Gordon and the scissors slip quietly up to his room; this is a private matter. He lifts out the tie, and cuts off the offending tail.

As long as he's been grown-up, in the middle of a long tedious sermon – some people do find sermons tedious – Gordon would turn to the man beside him and, in the interests of research, examine his tie. It was done in social gatherings too, and when he met a man he admired, after the handshake, there would be close scrutiny of the tie.

9

THE KINDNESS OF DENTISTS

OF all the woes that beset us in this rich and varied life, do the miseries of teeth come close to the top of the list? Not everybody suffers tooth anguish – how lovely and pleasant are their lives!

When he was young, Gordon's parents took him to the dentist the odd time. It hurt them as much as it hurt him. Gogo wasn't stoical, and Lydia was tender-hearted, and Will was a bit adrift in this area of horrid intimacy. Some teeth needed to come out, so the dentist administered an anaesthetic, enough to smother the little fellow's objections. Afterwards, very subdued and diminished, Gordon was brought home and tucked up in bed to recover. I'm pretty sure his parents looked at one another and vowed in perfect accord, *'Never, ever, again'.*

Then, tucked up in bed, Gordon started to vomit. Bother! He had been expected to recover rapidly, with Lydia pouring the balm of 'It's all finished now, darling' over him. He couldn't stop being sick, hateful for him, as well as wearying for his nurse-mother. Lydia phoned the doctor and he came to the rescue.

Gordon greeted him feebly from his bed. Good manners are important, even if you've lost your dignity, along with your last meal. That loss of dignity was forgotten, knocked for six by the next one. The doctor turned back the blankets, 'Now, Gordon will you just turn over, please?' And the doctor plunged a syringe into my brother's bare buttock. 'Ow!'

'Good man,' said the happy doctor, another tricky job well done.

'You'll feel better very soon.' As he packed away his loathsome instrument and prepared to go, my adorable brother reared up from his pillow of tears, stretched out his arm, shook the doctor's hand, and said unmistakably, in his own words, 'Thank you!'

Many years later, when he was grown up, Gordon's teeth caught up with him. I took him to the Health Board dentist, and we were told that what teeth he still had were in a deplorable state, and needed to be removed. This would be a Big Job, so Gogo was booked into St Columcille's Hospital in Loughlinstown, south of Dublin, as a day patient.

We drove to the hospital, nice and early. Gordon did not want to come. He gloomed and he huffed and he drooped and he shrank. He was trying, by will power, by the sheer weight of his funk, to slow us down, or miraculously to change my mind so that we could go home. What a lovely day we would have together!

When we arrived, of course we had to wait. Then the dental surgeon came and invited Gordon to go into The Operating Theatre with him. I had for years been in loco parentis for Gordon, even sometimes before his parents died. So I was invited - urged, the staff sensed rocks ahead - to go with him into the Op. room. An attendant helped him to get into a gown. A Gown! This was a gentleman who wore a business suit, with a good shirt and tie and cufflinks, every single day of his life.

'Good man, Gordon' said the hopeful nurse. 'Will you just take off your watch for me? I'll keep it safe.' This could only get worse. 'No, oh no! NO!' and more words to that effect. 'Ok,' the theatre nurse responded quickly. 'That's fine, you can keep your watch on. Now will you take off your glasses for me, and we'll put on this cap. Then you can lie down for me'. She showed him a sort of milkmaid's mob cap.

Without going into further painful detail, I can record that my brother had the general anaesthetic administered while he sat bolt upright on the operating table, wearing his watch and his glasses, and defiantly bareheaded.

We, the nurse and I, stood beside him, supporting him as he drifted and then subsided, pole-axed. He was laid down gently, and all his remaining teeth were taken out.

I waited in the Day Room, where he would stay in bed, under observation, until deemed fit enough to go home. When he began to wake up, I was called in to reassure him, and he was wheeled out to the bed that would be his for the rest of the day.

The bed was superfluous. 'We Do Not go to bed during the day, particularly when we are away from home. We will be going out to the car... in just a minute... when we start to feel a bit better.'

My brother wouldn't get into the bed, or allow himself to be helped, or persuaded. So, completely at the mercy of Gordon's tyranny, the nurse helped him into his clothes, and then seated him in a big armchair, which was brought in especially for him. They could have saved their energy. A bar stool would have been ok. For three hours Gordon sat on the edge of his throne, like a stylite on his pillar, but not so calm, muttering, picking at his fingers, looking at his watch every few minutes, and feeling dreadful. His mouth was bleeding and he was vomiting. He told me repeatedly, unceasingly, that it was time for us to go ''Ome'. Eventually, we left.

Being let out of prison had a remarkably uplifting effect on both of us. As we almost hedge-hopped home from the hospital, Gordon was full of excitement, and started making plans for the rest of the day.

'Mye mye' was the initial plan. 'I'm going to town.'

'When I use a word' Humpty Dumpty said in a rather scornful tone, 'it means just what I choose it to mean, neither more nor less.' When Lewis Carroll sent Alice through the looking glass, he set a happy precedent for people who love to make words do unexpected things.

We love Gordon-speak so much in our extended family that we freely use his unique vocabulary. It bonds us, our personal patois.

'I'm going to town!' he announced as we drove home. 'Well', said I, 'let's wait and see how you feel.' He didn't announce it any more, rather suggested it, then ruminated quietly on it. By the time we reached the house, the brave soldier was feeling miserable, and we went in and he was glad to be cosseted.

Some years later, when Gordon was in the care of the Peacehaven Trust, he was brought to a dentist. The outcome was a set of magnificent dentures. They restored the contours of his face, and they gave him a Bite. He willingly popped them in, on request, and five minutes later he took them out. Showing a good attitude, he brought his teeth in his travel bag when he went visiting, and he always brought toothpaste and brush.

For quite some time after the pesky dentures had been discarded, toothpaste and brush accompanied Gordon on his travels. Well, they are an essential part of a gentleman's personal kit, are they not? Irrespective of whether the gent possesses perfect, or any, teeth; even if the glories of his teeth have long ago departed.

Thoughts of Gordon, from Maggie

Margaret Murray Donohue lived across the road from Gordon, in Blackheath Gardens. Her parents' house became a second home for him. The following is her story of their long friendship. 'He's one of my oldest friends.' To Gordon she is simply Maggie Murray.

As a preface to Margaret's story, one incident illustrates Gordon's relationship with her family. The Murray house had been spruced up, especially the sitting room. To complete that room's refurbishment, the furniture had been comprehensively moved around. The family went out for a little while, leaving Gordon in charge. He stood in the lovely room, appalled by the desecration – all changed, changed utterly! Poor Maggie, and Maggie's mummymummy and daddydaddy. But they had overlooked their good friend's gift for fixing things.

When the family came home, Gordon greeted them happily and led them into the sitting room, where they were able to see that the furniture had all been restored to its original, proper place. Gordon had made everything all right.

This is what Maggie wrote:

When I think about who has had the most influence on my life Gordon springs to mind. We moved to 19 Blackheath Gardens across from Gordon's home when I was around 8 years old. He is eighteen months younger than me. I don't recall knowing him at that stage. My friends were the girls in the neighbourhood with whom I played dolls, and house, went skating etc. I think I was a little older when Gordon appeared on the scene. One day he was just there, and it was as though he had always been there.

My mother often recalled a few stories about him. As he hadn't started school he used to call in to see her, as she said 'appearing at her elbow'. One day she was wringing out sheets which she had steeping in the bath when Gordon decided to give her a hand. He wrung out a sheet, but not knowing where to put it flung it immediately back into the bath, delighted with himself. Task completed! She also recalled having her aunt and cousin to visit her on one occasion. She brought in the tea tray, set with three china cups, a cup each. Gordon went out to the kitchen and appeared back with a cup for himself, informing her by his actions that he should not be overlooked. Perhaps it was this that reminded her and us that Gordon was an equal.

He was a daily visitor to our home in number nineteen and warmly welcomed into it for years. He always referred to my parents as 'Mama 19' or 'Dada 19'. As there were four children in our house, two boys and two girls, it was a busy and boisterous place. He loved being in the middle of all the fun and activity. He especially loved a game that involved hiding a newspaper under a cushion, and the finder getting to chase the others with the folded paper and giving a smack on the bottom with the said folded paper. He kicked football with my brothers, enjoyed rough and tumble play and on occasions (reluctantly) helped my father in the garden. The TV was a big attraction as Gordon's family didn't have one at that time. He always had to say 'Ooooh' when he saw any couple kissing and would look to us for a reaction. My father almost had a similar response – he opened the newspaper to block anyone's view of the screen lest we would be corrupted by what was on view. Kissing!!!

Gordon has always been a social butterfly, loves being in the centre of social activity. When we got older and were able to drive he loved coming along in the car, especially visiting my Aunt, and doing the supermarket shopping. He loved to push the trolley. Back then and still today he loves to be introduced to new people, extending a warm hand to introduce himself.

Gordon would never stay for a meal, dashing home instead every evening for his dinner, having reminded us that the news was on. He regularly returned with his uneaten bread. He went to the top of the road each night to meet his father, and beamed all the way down with The Irish Times under his arm. He loved his Dad and copied him in so many ways.

I recall trying to teach him to write when I was about 12. We used to practise writing the name of his dog Bundy, with Gordon tracing over the letters or joining the dots. I'm not too sure how successful we were and if Gordon ever managed to write the name. I think that my mother told me that Gordon might not be as fast at learning as I hoped, so after persevering for a few days the task got dropped. I bet Gordon was delighted when I called it a day. Not that he ever complained. I think it was this that first put the idea of teaching or working with children with an intellectual disability into my head.

I also remember on one occasion Gordon was playing football with the lads on the road. He was the assistant goalie. But I got angry with them when they encouraged him to drop his trousers. He was happy to do this as he got a great reaction, being cheered on by the group. I was so cross with them and really let them know what I thought of them. I also told Gordon not to do this again for anyone. I'd say the lads were afraid of me after that despite the fact that I was about thirteen or fourteen. This incident taught me, even back then, that people could be mean and cruel to each other.

Gordon's parents were among the first people I informed when my father died suddenly, as we wanted him to know as soon as possible. He would have been due to come back over after his tea and it would have been too shocking for him. We gave him my father's watch as Gordon, who loved to tell the time, got on really well with him. Sometimes when Gordon, as a typical teenager, objected to carrying out certain tasks for his own parents, my father was great at encouraging him to do the right thing. Shoe polishing, shaving and the correct way to wear a tie spring to mind. They sat at night polishing their shoes, competing with each other for the best shine.

When Gordon would appear with a good five o'clock shadow, a gentle reminder about shaving worked a treat. Another time Gordon's parents were concerned as he was pulling down the knot of his tie and opening the top button, thereby looking less than his usual neat self. This was an additional change to his behaviour, as he used to spend time adjusting our school ties to ensure they were being worn properly. However, my father could not help in this regard, as this is how he sat at night to relax after his day's work, knot pulled down or open, and top button undone. Gordon was copying him.

Gordon's parents later moved to Greystones, and we kept up occasional contact. Mr Cochran called to visit me in Galway many years ago. His wife had died so life was very much changed, but Gordon was still very much present in his life. We agreed that Gordon might like a few days' break in Galway, and he has been coming to spend a few days every couple of months with my family since then.

He just blends in with us, like one of the family. History repeating itself in a fashion. We love him and always look forward to his visits. We love to hear his happy singing in the bathroom, the pleasure he gets from all things relating to the Royal Family, weddings, celebrations and Christmas. My children and our friends have grown up with him, and by this interaction they have learned to be accepting and understanding of people who are less able than themselves.

He travels to Galway by train and enjoys spinning around Galway on the buses before he makes his way to my home. He can tell me the bus routes he has been on each day.

Around town isn't a problem, but one day having heard Claregalway mentioned on the radio he said 'Gogo there'. I nearly passed peacefully away. He had taken the Tuam bus, crossed the busy N17, and taken the return bus to Galway. He has never lost the love of buses he has had since childhood.

Although he is a bit like a homing pigeon and arrives home for what should be dinnertime, there have been a few hiccups with him over the years. His 6 o'clock no longer corresponds to my 6 o'clock, so several heartbeats have been missed on many an occasion. When he finally arrives in, or we find him ambling along swinging his briefcase, beaming, he has the usual excuses – traffic, men and women, hungry, making their way home from work. It's always the fault of the train, bus or traffic. Gordon and his own actions are never to blame.

Years ago I brought him to Ballinasloe where I was working for the morning. As he had chosen to come home by train, I brought him to the station and instructed him in which direction his train would be travelling. Imagine my horror when at 6 p.m. I got a phone call from CIE in Westport saying Gordon was there. My mind was racing, wondering how I might resolve the situation. Luckily CIE was able to put him on a train to Athlone, and took care of him until they put him on a bus to Galway. He arrived at 10.30 p.m., beaming, having had a wonderful adventure. You could possibly have seen my teeth too, but not because I was laughing.

Gordon now carries a GPS so this has made tracing his wanderings less stressful.

He has slowed down a bit over the years, and now I hear 'Ah Maggie' more frequently if he is asked to give a hand with anything. In the past he loved to put away the shopping, put out rubbish and tidy up the papers. He still loves to go shopping, pushing the trolley and introducing himself to fellow shoppers. He loves to sort out the old papers in our house, and of course spends a fortune on buying daily papers about which he is very precious. I am always honoured when he allows me to read them.

He loves to keep himself busy sorting out his briefcase. He knows exactly what it contains, and would know if it had been disturbed. He dislikes it when it becomes battered. Recently there was an incident when a colleague remarked to me that she had seen Gordon with a laptop bag. I was sure she was mistaking it for a briefcase, until some weeks later, when searching for his laptop bag, my son discovered Gordon's battered briefcase hidden under a bed. Gordon had done a swap. I guess it hurt his pride and wallet when he had to return it, along with an apology and some lovely flowers. The next time he came it had all been forgotten.

That is one of his wonderful traits. He is so forgiving. He never holds a grudge or gets angry. He thinks his 'Ah Maggie' will get him away with anything, and it generally does.

I remember his father saying he realised he had raised a gentleman when Gordon was seen, head of the bus queue, holding back the passengers until those alighting were off, and he allowed the ladies in the queue to get on first.

I think that sums up Gordon. A joy, a gentleman, a positive influence in our lives, someone who is slowing down, but someone who still holds enthusiasm for all that is important in his life.

In Margaret's Christmas card to my family she wrote, about Gordon,

He gives us joy always.

On 2nd March 2012, she texted me,

Ruth is there any update on Gordon?
He's in my head as I face out to my retirement party,
because my field of work is all his fault. M.

10

THAT INVINCIBLE BUNCH

A toast to that invincible bunch...
Let's hear it for the ladies who lunch.

Stephen Sondheim

It was evening time in a home in South Dublin.

With care and concentration, a small middle-aged woman in the kitchen set up a supper tray with coffee and sandwiches. Then she brought it into a bedroom, where her older sister was waiting. They sat down together and ate the little feast and, happy to be together, they chatted about this and that. After the supper party, the younger woman, whose name was Eileen, knelt down to pray.

She carefully prayed for people she knew who were unwell, or who had problems, and she prayed for the people she loved. Many of these people never knew that they had been cared for in that special way, by Eileen.

The Lunch

In the mid-1970s two elderly ladies met in the Tara Towers Hotel, on the Merrion Road in Dublin. They chose a table, sat down and ordered tea. After the waiter brought the tea and walked away, one lady slipped a hand into her roomy bag and brought out a packet of small, perfectly formed sandwiches. As they had lunch, drinking tea and eating sandwiches, these women had a long and deeply personal conversation. Neither could possibly have foreseen the outcome of the meeting.

They were Mrs Lydia Cochran, whose son Gordon had been born with brain damage, and Miss Dorothy Blake, whose sister Eileen, had Down Syndrome. The long-term effect of a good sandwich cannot be underestimated.

Now, to clarify a point. Miss Blake was an elderly woman of grace and dignity. She wasn't generally called by her Christian name, except by people who had known her very well for a long time. We became friends, and I found myself calling her Dorothy. As my knowledge of her grew, I loved her more. But, giving her due honour for the purpose of this story, whose readers may not have been her intimates, I will refer to her as Miss Blake.

Eileen Blake lived with her sister after their parents' deaths. Miss Blake had retired. Their sister Dr Lois Blake was approaching retirement from her position as a medical consultant in England.

Miss Blake and Mrs Cochran wanted to found a 'family-type' home for adults who at that time were described as being 'mentally handicapped'. That is, they seriously intended to do this; they could not imagine any obstacle that would stop them. If it was the right thing to do, and if it was supported by prayer, how could such a project fail?

There were organisations in Ireland providing resources for people with an intellectual disability, day-schools and workshops, also full-time and weekly residential facilities. At that time the residences or Homes tended to be quite large. That was the most financially effective way to provide the varied levels of support the residents needed, and the care was often excellent. Miss Blake and my mother in their dream saw something different.

Their model would be a home with maybe six or 8 residents, with a married couple running it, filling the roles of houseparents. Residents who lived there would attend workshops run by other organisations, where that was appropriate.

The other distinctive characteristic of this new Home would

be that the staff and the management committee, later the Board of Directors, would be Evangelical Christians. This wasn't a campaign to proselytise, it was a very simple expression of the faith-based lives of the founding group. Earlier in this story I've described some of the activities and attitudes of my family and their fellow-Christians. God's love was part of their lives, it defined them. An applicant for a place in the new home would never be, and has never been, rejected on grounds of religion or belief system. They are honoured, as equal individuals.

A committee was formed, of which I was part. We wrote letters to newspapers and to friends. We asked for advice from experts, we broke new ground, we took risks that we weren't even aware of. We advanced step by step. The name, Peacehaven, was chosen for the organisation before there was any money to buy a house, before the founders began to receive financial and administrative support from professional people, from Health Board officers, friends or charities. Lydia suggested taking the name from a couple of verses in the Bible, in the Old Testament book of Isaiah, chapter 32. Verses 17 and 18 were what caught her attention.

> The fruit of righteousness will be peace, the effect of righteousness will be quietness and confidence for ever. My people will live in peaceful dwelling places, in secure homes, in undisturbed places of rest.

'Righteousness' was not to be confused with self-righteousness. We were fully aware of our faults, and we deplored them.

After we began to receive significant financial support, we house-hunted in various areas. We bought a pair of semi-detached houses in Greystones, numbers 1 and 2 Hillside Estate, which were combined to form one residence, and Miss Blake and I had the time of our lives selecting wallpaper, paints, fittings, curtains, furniture. We were like a young couple furnishing their first nest.

The Outcome of the Lunch

Skipping forward about thirty-five years, the Peacehaven Trust Limited now owns three homes in Greystones. The staff are highly qualified, and they're no longer viewed as substitute parents. The Peacehaven Trust has at all times been accorded the respect and the support of the then Eastern Health Board and, more recently, of The Health Service Executive.

The story of the conception, the birth, growth and maturing of Peacehaven would, maybe will, fill a fat volume. We've had challenging, worrying, uplifting, exciting, and – human nature being what it has to be – hilarious times.

One of our early public meetings, to launch the work, was held in the Adelaide Road Presbyterian Church, which was Kindly Lent. We were thrilled when lots of people came. Dr Barbara Stokes and Dr Vincent Molony were our speakers. It was summer, and quite bright as the meeting started. Then the day began to grow dim, we realised the auditorium was looking gloomy, and we went to switch on the lights. We couldn't find the switches, not even one single switch. Gloom changed to deep twilight, and as we searched every wall and doorway, nook and cranny, we were beginning to panic, thinking of desperate measures such as flying out to a late-opening shop for candles or for bagloads of torches, when someone found the switches and we had light!

Our committee meetings were held in the city church, Merrion Hall, where the Missionary Conference had been an annual delight for Gordon. We met on the lower ground floor, in what I believe was the Elders' Room. Like a slightly shabby Board Room, with a central table. There were portraits of mature kindly men on the walls. I think my husband's grandfather may have been among them. There was another room nearby, a humble one, with no discernible function, which we were given at other times for our meetings. Slightly fusty rooms, in a tired, old, much-loved building.

Merrion Hall was eventually transformed into the Davenport Hotel. One day John Giles, a founding Peacehaven Trust committee member, found himself at a meeting in the Davenport, in just the area where we used to meet in the little room. It was unrecognisable of course, but John mischievously asserted that it smelled *exactly* the same.

Another outcome of the invincible ladies' lunch was that in October 1978, my parents and Gordon moved to live in Greystones. They bought number 9 Hillside, close to the Peacehaven home. These houses were brand new – we had bought the Peacehaven houses off the plans.

My mother read in her Streams in the Desert diary,

> The Lord longs to be gracious to you; he rises to show you compassion. For the Lord is a God of justice. Blessed are all who wait for him! Isaiah 30:18.
>
> Don't say, child of God, that the sun is quenched because the cloud has hidden it. No, He is behind the cloud, preparing Summer for you. When He appears, you will have joy in the Lord, and you will rejoice with joy unspeakable.

(I've paraphrased the 'Streams' extract because it's written in the style of nearly one hundred years ago.)

And along the side of the page Lydia wrote,

> I read this when there had been heavy rain, low clouds. Then I looked out the French window & such a sight I saw – bright sunshine on drenched grass & trees, and the colours as though they had been painted, fuchsia vivid red & grass liquid green! In dear Blackheath Gardens.

My wonderful, funny mother also tucked into the pages a leaf from a wall calendar with another Scripture quote, from the book of Nehemiah,

Yea, forty years didst thou sustain them in the wilderness.

That quotation was followed by an emphatic exclamation mark.

The move from Clontarf to Greystones was not perfectly organised. I think my parents were (still) financially skint, and in trying to save money, they did a sort of informal 'flit', as though making a quick escape. Keith and I drove a packed car to Greystones, to help them to get installed.

We worked hard, and it was late and dark as we left, and when I was scurrying to the car on the new road which was littered with building debris, I landed on a plank which had a nail sticking up out of it. The nail went through my shoe, and into my foot. An odd sensation, not painful, but horribly shocking. We decided to go straight to the hospital at Loughlinstown. But at that time I was the nominated driver for our family. And I couldn't drive because of the dirty great hole in my foot.

Not long before, Keith had had the first of two operations on his eyes to repair detached retinas. It was a pretty invasive procedure at that time, and he wasn't supposed to lift anything or exert himself in any way for some weeks. Particularly, he was instructed not to drive. So for these weeks I had been occupying his seat.

Shrugging off doctor's orders, my hero resumed his driver's seat and we went to the hospital and I got cleaned up and injected, and we arrived safely home.

For a long time my sister Dorothy has been missing from the story. As soon as she was grown-up Dorothy moved away, to live in Ballydehob in County Cork to become a weaver, then to Wales, and to parts of England. After coming home for several short periods, she went away for good, with a partner from Dublin. For a long time, many years, we didn't know where she was or if she was alive. Our mother sorrowed for Dorothy. She had disappeared, and our mother mourned the loss of the copper-knobbed girl she had loved. She did dream for a while, distressingly, that Dorothy had dyed her hair black.

Dorothy, by now Helga, began eventually to phone me from her home in the South of England. She had been in poor health for some years, supported and cared for by her partner, John. My sister and I gradually formed a new friendship. I made several very happy visits to them, and we enjoyed each other's company.

It's about Gordon, actually

Living in Greystones for my parents and Gordon was very strange, in some unexpected ways. The thinking behind the move was that if Gordon was ever to go up the road to live in Peacehaven, which was his parents' dream, he could get used to it while living close by. That proved to be a ridiculous notion! There were several reasons why it was so.

Why would he want to spend time in another house up the road, when he had a perfectly good home down the road? There was another reason.

Although he had quantities of fond acquaintances Gordon had never made close friends of his own, outside family, church and his very special Maggie Murray. He frankly didn't understand the people who had come to live in the Peacehaven home, and he didn't feel inclined to try. They didn't share his interests, and they didn't work in offices.

Lydia found Greystones very hard, and she was homesick for Clontarf. She would have agreed wholeheartedly with Margaret Attwood's comment that 'the threshold of a new house is a lonely place'.

There were other drawbacks to Greystones. Nobody had told my parents about the mist, or fog, which seemed at times to muffle the place. Lydia hated that. They had loved going to Greystones for holidays, from Belfast. Lydia discovered that Greystones was delightful to visit, and a charming place to leave behind when home was calling you.

She missed Dublin. How can you pop into Grafton Street to meet Ruth for coffee, if you live in Greystones? And she was amazed that the lovely women of Greystones, who welcomed her warmly and became her friends, were not constantly longing and planning to go to Town! Bray Head, instead of being a benign hump just to the north, began to look like Everest.

Will settled in happily. He bought a greenhouse, erected it himself, and dreamed of harvesting tomatoes, and growing tender plants. As well, he worked for a while as a volunteer with a mission organisation in Dalkey, teaching Bible correspondence courses to people in an African country,

Gordon started sheltered work in Sunbeam House, in the Dargle Centre in Bray, doing some sort of simple assembly job. There was much kindness, and great good humour, but he was very much out of his milieu. Everything was different and bewildering. A photograph taken at that time shows him working, facing a wall. There may have been some form of music playing, to make a cheerful atmosphere, quite a happy racket probably, and he certainly wasn't used to that. Home life was quiet. There was no din.

In 1983, when shopping in the village, Will fell. Lydia noted in her Streams-diary,

Beloved fell. Trust needed.

Of course, he protested that he was all right. Later it was found that he had hurt his wrist, but astonishingly, though he had also damaged his hip, in standing up so quickly he had corrected the misalignment, and it stuck or got wedged into the right position. Anyway, it mended. There was no lasting damage. He found his brief time in hospital – his first time ever – a brand new, interesting experience, and he was bowled over by the nurses' kindness, especially in caring for some male patients who were definitely unlovely.

One life-changing summer day, Gordon went to the beach with a group from work. He was severely sun-burned, and stayed miserably in bed, in pain. The burns healed, and Gordon refused to get out of bed. He simply stayed in bed, cowering if urged to get up, and crying if he was challenged. Lydia would climb the stairs to see him, and sometimes he would be invisible, weeping, with the blankets over his head. His mother was irrationally afraid that if she called the doctor he would whisk Gordon off to a psychiatric hospital.

Eventually, the local GP was called, and after grave consideration, he gave his verdict. Gordon's parents were instructed to tell him that he could stop going to work, he need never go again. He could get up and do just whatever he liked.

Gordon got up out of bed, dressed himself and started his new life.

Heuston Station

Michael and Maggie in Galway

DAD

TEA IN THE
SIGNAL BOX

Brendan and Pauline

PEARSE STATION

Donnybrook Bus Garage

KEITH

Ruth

FRED
AND
RUTH

The Wicklow People

11

MY BROTHER, THE ATHLETE

The Special Olympics. University College Dublin, 1985
A massive section of Irish people found itself with an unquenchable idiotic smile on its face this week. It seemed as though something long neglected in the Irish spirit had found its outlet, had been honoured and fulfilled. Years from now, sociologists may pinpoint this as the time when a country recovered its soul.
The Irish Times, Saturday Weekend Review

Yes, it was wonderful. That charming bit of hyperbole from The Irish Times recognised that something new and lovely had happened.

Gordon was 32 when he went to UCD for the first and last time, to take part in the European Special Olympics, and to live there with the other athletes. He wasn't noticeably impressed by sport. The problem with my very adult brother was that he regarded all sport as being something children do, beneath his dignity and completely pointless. If he was invited to join a game, he might give it one try, out of courtesy. Then he would back off, buzzing with embarrassment, and saying Pshaw! Well, that's what he thought he was saying.

His new sports kit was fine, in shades of blue. He was entered for the events in which he was least likely to disgrace himself. They included the Softball Throw, and the 50m Dash. At all the events were 'huggers', volunteers who encouraged the competitors and then joyfully hugged each one, on the dubious basis that everybody had won. Gordon was awarded several medals. As a matter of principle, the Special Olympics did not announce that anyone had lost a race.

The organisers, the supporters, the volunteers, the financial benefactors, the celebrities, the huggers... all poured themselves into making the Games a success. Ted Kennedy was there; his sister, Eunice Kennedy Shriver, had founded the Games.

Photos of Gordon at the event show him, surrounded by beautiful young volunteers, looking befuddled. What on earth was he thinking? Many of his workmates would have been entered for the Games, for good and well-considered reasons. But I believe that Gordon would have been so much more happy if he had been left out.

The clarity of this realisation connects me with some more recent criticisms of the whole movement, one being that it's planned and run by people who do not have an intellectual disability, for those who do. It is necessary to have that disability to qualify for entry. No other criteria apply. The requirement that principles of equality must inform social attitudes can lead to some bizarre conclusions. The later emphasis on supporting or legislating for equal rights is not the unique remedy for a disordered society.

If there is prejudice – for whatever reason – against a sector of the population, gathering all the members of that sector together for a specially tailored event isn't going to overcome prejudice. The people thus gathered can become members of a Category. The lovely huggers at the Games could be seen as patronising. Tiny children are hugged when they toddle as fast as they can. Anne, the British Princess Royal, was amazed at the very idea that all children want to be cuddled by a complete stranger. Adults are not normally subjected to organised embraces. They can choose not to be enfolded in the arms of someone they don't know. Athletes whose bodies are disabled, but whose minds are not so, can decide for themselves. They are very different from athletes who have an intellectual disability. It's a brave equal-opportunity theorist who steps into that complicated arena.

Every decade, or even every year, finds altered thinking on these issues. At the time of which I write, 1985, people did their very best, with honourable intent. They made a lot of people very, very happy.

Today, instead of urging a person with an intellectual disability to do something, or – horrors! – instructing them to do it, a social care worker will give them all the information they need, and will support them in making a decision. It's the best, most respectful way, but perfect outcomes cannot ever be guaranteed. Equality of opportunity is a splendid aspiration, and an absolute labyrinth of complexity, impossible to achieve. We are, after all, magnificently, peerlessly, unevenly, human.

Un vrai Flâneur!

In the morning Gordon assembled himself for the day, suit, shirt, tie, raincoat if necessary, and briefcase. The need for newspapers would be satisfied later, probably at Bray Railway Station. If he was unfortunately without an umbrella, he would keep his eyes peeled, and before long he'd find the umbrella that some absolute scatterbrain had left on the train, and it would become his. He didn't wear the raincoat; it hung negligently over his arm. It was an accessory.

After breakfast he strolled away, to the bus which would bring him to Bray, or – a longer walk – to the Greystones railway station, from where he also ended up in Bray. Having been given some money, he used it for its primary purpose, to buy a couple of newspapers in Eugene's shop. (I'm sorry to say that Keith used to make him chuckle by asking if he got his hair cut in Eugene's.) I suspect that he browsed and rummaged at the counters, he was a born rummager, and maybe he took more than he was entitled to. You see, he needed the papers, as other lords of the business world needed their favourite stimulant. The staff at the station were very kind to him, I think he had many cups of tea, and maybe a bite of something, as he briefly became an honorary Irish Rail staff member. Then a Dublin-bound train would roll in, and, fully focused on the day ahead, Gordon would wave, board, and be gone.

Mostly his parents didn't know where he had been when he returned, exhausted, after a heavy day.

He made friends whom we never met, and he became well known, so that if one of us was with him, it was quite usual to have complete strangers calling out 'Hello Gordon!' The Greystones station staff were like brothers to him and they've given him gifts, which I don't propose to list here, that were normally only worn or used by those in Irish Rail's employ. He had Christmas cards from them – Happy Christmas Gordon and a happy New Year, from ... and a list of names. I'm aware that Gordon's friendship is a mixed blessing, and I've never heard about, but can imagine, the papers and documents he must inevitably have stolen from station offices. We couldn't train it out of him. These men helped to celebrate his birthdays, and he brought cake to their office, to party with them.

From time to time my brother was denied access to Irish Rail offices, because of the way documents flew into his hands and vanished into his briefcase. Not only documents gravitated to Gogo. On one particular day he was with his friends in a Railway Station, where he was always made welcome. There were no interesting documents lying around – they must have tidied everything up, what a swizz! – so he wandered round, arriving at the staff members' room, where he spent a few minutes researching. Nobody bothered about him. The men viewed him as one of themselves, with some variations.

In due course, Gordon reappeared, picked up his briefcase and other bits and pieces, saluted briskly and strode off.

'Who's been eating my dinner?' One of the team had laid his

dinner out, and gone away for a moment. Coming back, appetite well sharpened, he arrived at what was left of his meal. Gordon had eaten most of it. Dinner was a poor substitute for business papers, but Gordon was a realist, and for the present it filled a gap.

He was particularly blessed in having a brother-in-law whose career was, by happenstance, spent in Irish Rail. Could anything be more perfect? So, in 1985 when Keith, Technical Manager for the Company, went to Rathdrum, far south in Co Wicklow, to investigate an urgent problem, who should he see but Gordon comfortably socialising with the staff members in the station.

His travels did include a crisis or two. He was never actually lost, but his choices of destination sometimes surprised him. Greater celebrities than he have got stuck and called for help. G. K. Chesterton, calling for help, sent a telegram to his wife, AM IN WOLVERHAMPTON STOP WHERE OUGHT I TO BE. People didn't use question marks in telegrams, every letter and mark counted and had to be paid for.

There was a bomb scare at Dublin's Connolly Station, at the time when Gordon lived with us. He had been out far west of Dublin, on the Maynooth line, and was coming home. The incoming train was stopped at Clonsilla, with Gordon inside it. He may have been visiting Mullingar. However, he (and a lot of other unfortunate people, of whom we know nothing) was stuck. We nearly burned out the phone, making calls everywhere. By the Grace of God, and the kindness of man, we got him home eventually, absolutely full of his wonderful adventure.

Buses were less exciting – no bomb scares on buses, that we heard of – but they were good for getting around. One summer evening, again when Gordon was staying with us, he came home for dinner, and he was restless, because it was still bright outside. 'Bus bus', he announced. It was about 7.30, so I said 'Ok, go into town, but come home quickly; don't stay out late!' I felt like my mother.

Off he went. At times just thinking of his busy schedule made me tired. We had a peaceful evening, and I dozed on the sofa. There were running steps coming downstairs. Virginia came in, asking, 'Do you know that Gogo hasn't come home?' Everybody had gone to bed, except me, and Gordon, who was still out, and it was nearly midnight. The last bus would have gone.

I set off in the car. My idea was to go directly to the 15B terminus on College Street, where Gordon would normally get the bus to our home in Rathfarnham. If he wasn't there I would drive towards home as slowly as possible along the route the bus would take, thinking that if there was no bus, Gogo might have started to walk home along that route. So I went into town, drove through Westmoreland Street, and curled round to the right into D'Olier Street towards the terminus. As I approached I could see a Nitelink bus at the stop, waiting for late revellers. It felt very late, and lonely.

Gordon was standing at the bus stop. Would he have stayed there till the early morning service started? Would the Garda have scooped him up, and kept him safe until someone sent out an SOS? Waiting quietly in the city long after midnight, still with all his paraphernalia, how vulnerable he was. Speechless, in the face of anyone who might accost him.

Brendan Jordan is a great friend of Gordon's. He and his wife Pauline have been regular guests at Gordon's birthday parties. To be my brother's friend, Brendan's credentials were just right; he was one of the Irish Rail Operating Staff on the Wexford line. What an enviable job. One day, Brendan needed to go to Dublin Airport, and he had the happy thought of inviting Gordon to go with him. The Airport would be a new interest. It was going to be a lovely experience for Gordon, a change from endless buses and trains. An eye-opener!

They arrived at their destination and went in to Arrivals, my brother striding in as though he owned the place. Well, he almost did. On every hand people gave him a wave, called 'Hello Gordon', and generally responded to him as if he was Airport Man, instead of Railway Man, or more humbly Bus Man. Kind Brendan looked at his celebrity friend in a new light.

I had no idea of Gordon's Airport Junkets when I went, around the mid 1990s, to meet Virginia and Jeremy, our daughter and son on their return from Paris. Abigail, our second daughter, who was married in 1992, missed some of the Gogo shenanigans we were blessed with.

I went to the Arrivals, sat down in the front row of seats and took out my book. There was a familiar gutsy chuckle and, lighting up the Arrivals Hall with his glowing face, Gordon sat down beside me. Each was equally astounded to see the other. We were enchanted! And Virginia and Jeremy got a celebrity welcome home.

When I was thinking about writing Gordon's story, I emailed the Airport's Public Relations office, asking if Gordon was known to them. A reply came from the Arrivals Hall. The staff certainly knew him. Sadly, when he suggested that some of the highly desirable timetables might be available, to enrich his briefcase collection, they had none to give him.

Encore le Flâneur

Am I showing disrespect (the absolute worst social sin these days) to Gordon by tucking in a word or two of French? Since he can't speak much of any language, he certainly wouldn't either appreciate it or be offended by it. But if he ever gets to see this – his – book, I'll show the exotic words to him, and he'll be happy. I know.

Every now and then a story filtered through to Greystones or to Rathfarnham of some sighting of Gordon.

He was seen travelling in the back cab of a DART train. How did he wangle that? The notion of one day stalking him crossed our minds, but we never did.

Two members of the family did see a typical Gordon incident, just by happy chance. Keith's brother Stuart and his wife Sharon were on the Rosslare train, and spied Gordon in the back driver's cab. Not, of course, on his own. After a while – being chatty is so tiring – his fellow traveller, an Irish Rail staff member (co-worker?) came out of the cab, and disappeared up the train. Back he came after a few minutes, carrying two cups of steaming tea, and the two friends settled down, in the middle of a busy day, to a well-earned tea-break.

The following brief cameo was played on a railway platform at Lansdowne Road, in Dublin. Our hero was waiting for a train, standing by himself, aloof, perhaps glancing at his watch in a concerned manner. He hated waiting, and it's what he spent most of every day doing. So he may have looked a trifle impatient. Another waiting passenger looked at the distinctive man, impressed by his dignity and the touch of eccentricity. He turned to the person standing near him. 'You see that man over there, standing near the edge of the platform? The little man with the thick glasses – he always has a briefcase.' They both gazed at the small man. 'Well', said the one who seemed to know everything, 'he's a very famous scientist, absolutely brilliant. You can tell by looking at him, can't you?' They agreed that they could.

A much later story shows Gordon's impeccable sense of place. My father and he were living with us, and my dad suggested taking a run in the car to Blessington, where Lydia's childhood best friend Gladys still lived. So off we drove. We had left Tallaght far behind and were approaching Brittas when Gordon, who knew nothing about Geography or the beauty of maps, looked to the left, where between the shrubby trees water gleamed. 'The sea!' he announced, very interested. 'No, not the sea, Gogo,' I replied, 'it's a big lake, in the middle of the fields'. A bored mutter greeted that.

We had a lovely time with Gladys, Mrs Byrne, and then we started for home. It was wintry, getting dark. We drove peacefully as darkness began to fall. Then Gordon roused himself, looked to the right, pointed into the gloom, and confidently told us that we were passing the lake. He was perfectly right.

The quality of mercy... a man whom I will call Guardian Angel, for this tale, had lived in the Peacehaven Home in Greystones at one time, and he knew Gordon well. Then he moved into his own flat. One day he was sitting in a café close to O'Connell Street in the centre of Dublin, enjoying a coffee. He was absent-mindedly watching the people walking past, when he focused on Gordon. To his consternation he saw a small group of youths following Gordon, laughing at him in mockery. This looked bad.

Guardian Angel jumped up, hurried out into the street and caught up with Gordon. 'Hello Gordon! I'm having coffee in there,' indicating the café, 'would you like to come in and have coffee with me?' Gordon, who had no notion that Guardian Angel wanted to protect him, refused, explaining that he was in a hurry, pressure of work etc etc, and couldn't spare the time to socialise, even with an erstwhile friend.

There was a family death. My aunt, my father's sister-in-law, died. Her funeral was in the church shared by the Methodist and Presbyterian congregations in Sandymount, in Dublin. Keith went to work that morning, planning to go to the church later on. Gordon was enthusiastic about going. If there weren't any weddings on the horizon, a funeral was a good substitute, and always an opportunity to exchange warm handshakes, to catch up with new friends. He refused to go with any of the family. He was living with us at the time, and he decided to go to 'work' early, as usual, and make his own way to the church. But he'd never been there, and he didn't know Sandymount. We did not want him to get lost, not for his sake, and especially not for ours. Chasing him up was so tedious.

From troubles of the world, one can profitably turn to newspapers, but on other occasions, I love to turn to maps. I would turn to ducks, the inspiration for that perfect poem, except that we have none. We do have quantities of maps. What's the point of reading about far-off places if you can't turn up a map and trace the rivers and roads and mountains, and *be there?* (Yes, I know

Google will take you walking through the streets, and flying above the trees, but this was then.)

I showed Gordon the Dublin Street Atlas. We turned up the page for Sandymount. I told him which bus to take – he knew where the city stop was, of course – and we traced its journey to the nearest point to the church, pointing out junctions, where the sea was, what places to watch out for, and he enjoyed this bit of mutual study. Then I took a nice fresh bit of paper and wrote down who he was, and where he was going, asking people to direct him if he went off-course. It was particularly addressed to the bus conductor, asking him to tell Gordon where to get off. The piece of paper was to be kept safe; I told him to show it to people if he needed help. I think I put our phone number on it; I hope I did.

Keith drove to the church in very good time, parked, and went in. He chose a seat, and as he sat down Gordon turned towards him, and offered a welcoming hand.

If Shakespeare had known my brother, he might have saved these words to describe him:

> He's gentle; never schooled and yet learned; full of noble device; of all sorts enchantingly beloved; ... so much in the heart of the world, and especially of my own people, who best know him.

When we met friends, they never told us 'I saw Bono in Bewley's!' or 'Gaybo was strolling in Grafton Street!'

They said 'I saw Gordon today'.

12

GREYSTONES

AFTER Lydia and Will and Gordon moved to Greystones, the place became our focus, for several reasons. My parents and Gordon were making a home, and Peacehaven was becoming a home.

The Peacehaven committee met regularly, at first in Dublin, then in Greystones. Over time the organisation grew and changed to meet society's changing principles of Social Care. It was the most thrilling and challenging adventure.

During the 1980s Lydia became forgetful. Forgetfulness is a difficulty, but as well as that her hearing got worse and she became nearly stone deaf. A pair of hearing aids helped, and we became used to the tricks, speaking directly to her, e-nun-ci-at-ing everything clearly, emphasising consonants, using face and body to illustrate what we were talking about.

She was on the Peacehaven committee, and I have a special memory. At that time Michael Croly was manager of the home, and he met in committee with us. When he participated in the discussions, he would turn towards my mother and make sure she was able to see, as well as to hear, his words. It was unobtrusively and gracefully done, and very kind.

Lydia's heartbeat had become erratic; she had 'palpitations' which sort of froze her in her chair, frightening and distressing. Gordon became aware of this. When he saw that Mummymummy was unwell, he would go over to her, and murmur softly and gently place his fingers on the side of her neck. He didn't know that a hectic pulse was there, but this was something that Dad did, so it was right for the son to do it.

At one time when she was particularly unwell, Keith and I took her to our home in Rathfarnham, where I tucked her into bed and looked after her.

As I made her comfy, on a whim I asked her if she ever missed her own mother. Of course she did. Her mother had died before Lydia was thirty. Knowing that we cannot communicate with people who have died, nonetheless, Lydia told me that sometimes when she was praying, she used to informally ask God to pass on a little message to her mum. It's not recommended in Scripture, but the Father knew His child and comforted her.

As a mother comforts her child, so will I comfort you.

Another reason for Greystones to be a focus for us was that it became a safe refuge when we needed one. Keith and I and our children went to stay often with my parents. After the two operations, four months apart, to repair detached retinas, Keith was ill for nearly a year, during 1979. Part of his healing was the comfort and simplicity of visiting Nana's and Papa's home.

My husband recovered, went back to work and was promoted! This isn't the place to list the great kindnesses, the many gifts of money and offers of help, and the love that was poured over us during that year. I have my own diary, kept safe.

Lydia wrote in Streams in the Desert,

We could not sell our house [in Clontarf] in November 1978, & didn't see the reason why. Sold it now – much better price. Our Father knew we'd need the money to help Ruth & Keith. Keith not back in office till end of October. What a wonderful Lord we have.

Ring Out Wild Bells!

Oh, we loved Christmas, Dorothy and I and Gordon! When we were children the real excitement began early on the morning of Christmas Eve, when honorary 'Uncle' Henry came down to us in his big car, with the loan of a steamer, a most useful three-storey set of cooking pots. Lydia would use it to augment her own pots and pans to cook dinner the next day. After taking delivery of the steamer we made our Christmas Eve pilgrimage to town.

There were always up to half a dozen other family members visiting us on The Day, and it was the most homely event. One of the side dishes at dinner was a bunch of celery sticks standing in a glass of water. We never had them at any other time, and I don't remember anybody eating them. I certainly didn't. What's raw celery for? Could a fashion for celery on the Christmas table have originated from The Dead, Joyce's story of an Epiphany supper party? It was written the year after my mother was born, and maybe it was widely read.

'Along with a great ham, custard sprinkled with nutmeg, chocolates... a glass vase in which stood some tall celery sticks.'

One of the party people never ate sweets, so the celery was left for him – a miserable alternative!

'Freddy Malins ate a stalk with his pudding – for his blood.'

We had oodles of home-made crepe paper decorations, always pink and green, to tone with – to go with – the drawingroom, and a big tree. Our parents threw a sparkle of good cheer over everything for us.

Santa Claus visited us. On one Christmas night he left me a brand new bookcase! My serious Book Hoarding Obsession was developing nicely. But my manners were not. I complained about the bookcase, because it looked unusual, and the varnish was an unorthodox reddish colour.

Another Christmas tradition was set when I was long grown

up, and Keith and I with our children lived in Rathfarnham. My parents and Gordon came to us. They arrived on Christmas Eve, with everything they might possibly need, in case we were snowed in for months. Lydia viewed our home as being almost in the Dublin mountains, and therefore dangerously vulnerable to snow. When visiting, she always wore her furry boots and wrapped herself in mohair scarves. They brought bags and holdalls and travel rugs, and all sorts of food, and a posy of Christmas Roses – the flowers, not the chocolates. Who would choose a chocolate if one could have instead one of these exquisite pearl-white blooms, with its lambent face modestly dipped? They stayed with us, all of us having such a happy time, with small treats, trips out for coffee, and ceaseless chat, until New Year's Eve, when they came with us to a party in our church. From there they went home to Greystones. The next day, every year, I went down with flu.

One Christmas Day saw my mother, sitting in our kitchen, begin to cry. Her whole body was flooded with tears, the weight of grief drowning her. Dorothy, Gordon, loneliness, Keith's long illness, loss of her own mother, Will's business problems, Greystones, Virginia's long illness – her weeping was like death. She couldn't stop till she was wept dry, and in weakness and pain. We supported her, made tea for her, held her. She spent a lot of that day snuggled in bed, and she recovered and took hold again of the shield of faith, and went forward.

It's a great life if you don't weaken, a Marriage and a Death.

John Buchan, Mr Standfast

On 28th December 1991 our daughter Abigail and her lovely boyfriend Ciaran announced their engagement, to our great joy. They planned their wedding for the 18th July, the following year. We are incurably DIY people, so we planned what we would do. I started making wedding dresses for her and for her four bridesmaids. They were to be her sister Virginia and her best friend from schooldays, and two little cousins. And I needed to make a dress for myself. I started assembling cake ingredients.

I was having physiotherapy for a frozen shoulder.

Virginia had been unwell for some time, and in February a group of people came from our church to pray with her. Jeremy was preparing for the Leaving Cert exam.

Dementia had taken hold of my mother, gently, taking away her memory. I would phone her in the morning and say that I would be down to see her later. She'd be very happy. When I arrived, an hour later, Lydia would open the door and exclaim, astonished to see me, 'Oh, isn't the Lord very good to me!'

Dementia is heartbreaking, of course, and there are moments of high comedy too. When my dad, in full possession of all his wits, and perfectly healthy, would ask a simple question, his adoring, but exasperated wife would sigh, 'I never thought I'd be married to an *old man.*'

Sitting with Will at breakfast one morning in February, Lydia was felled by a stroke. Gordon had left for work and would be out all day. Will phoned me, saying that she was going to be brought to Loughlinstown Hospital. I dropped everything and sped to Loughlinstown. I was there before the ambulance arrived, in time to meet the stretcher on which she was wheeled in. I went over, identified myself to the paramedics, and with great seriousness, as I laid my hand on her head, I explained 'I love her. You see I've known her *all my life*'.

In due course, my dad went home to be there for Gordon.

I forgot about physiotherapy, and the shoulder hasn't felt a twinge since. The body prioritised.

My mother could not eat or drink, so she was tube fed. She did not like this, so the nurses made a big wadded mitt on the hand that still had movement, to stop her batting the tubes out of position. After some time, a couple of weeks, I walked into my mum's room. The offensive tube was out, her hand was free, and a nurse was sitting beside the bed, feeding her custard with a spoon! She could swallow. Oh, such a flood of joyful tears! The nurse was beaming with delight. When I left I went straight to my mother-in-law, Doris, and we rejoiced together.

Lydia was moved to a nursing home in Bray. As a result of the stroke, she seemed to understand very little. She didn't speak or communicate. Mostly she was full of smiles. Strokes do funny things to people, so on other days she wept and howled, deeply distressed.

My dad talked with us about the future, concerns about their house, about wills, money, business matters, and Gordon's future. I don't think we decided anything, though all these matters needed attention. Gordon's future was in a vague way expected to involve Peacehaven.

On my mum's birthday, the 8th May, we brought a cake in, and she tried to join us in singing Happy Birthday to herself, and essayed to eat the whole cake. Will went to visit Dorothy/ Helga, in Hampshire where she and John lived. Gordon came to stay with us.

Abigail and Ciaran were radiantly married on Saturday 18th July, as planned. Well, one plan misfired a little. Her best friend, who had married the previous year, was pregnant, and I had had fun designing and making a maternity bridesmaid dress. But she couldn't wait, and she gave birth to a daughter just before Abigail's wedding, so she never got to wear the dress.

We decorated the church with flowers. Abigail made all the bouquets on the wedding morning, and decorated the beautiful Classic Car in which our friend John Horan would drive her. Our friends, David and Anne Hull, who came to the wedding from Northern Ireland, were wonderfully supportive, driving me to the church, and the next day taking me to visit my mother in Bray. She was now permanently in bed, situated close to the nurses' station for observation, motionless, deaf to everything. There, my friends prayed with us. I felt rested, like a child with grown-ups in control.

Where, O death, is your sting?

On Thursday, five days after the wedding, my dad phoned, saying that the nursing home had advised us to come in. So we went and sat with my mother. Such stillness, such tiny breaths. We chatted quietly as we waited for a long time, then I listened, and said, 'I think she has died.' Before we left, Will bent over, kissed Lydia, and murmured 'Goodbye, Beloved'.

> In righteousness I shall see your face; when I awake,
> I shall be satisfied with seeing your likeness.
>
> **Psalm 17**

Driving back to Greystones, we stopped for a while, and we opened and read a letter that Lydia had been writing on and off for years, for this purpose. It was full of thankfulness to God, and loving messages to everybody, and included a plea that members of her extended family would put their trust in Jesus, if they did not already belong to Him. We discussed what to do next, and my dad was sensitive of my loss, quoting from the book of Joshua,

> '... You will know which way to go, since
> you have never been this way before'.

I dropped him home to start organising the funeral, and I popped up to Greystones Tesco for some biscuits and little cakes. As Will had said to me, people might call, and we'd need something nice to give them. At the supermarket I met a friend, whom I knew from church and from involvement with children's camps. 'Hello', she cried, full of bonhomie, 'how are you?' 'I'm very well', I answered, 'my mother has just died'.

When Gordon came home that evening, my dad had to explain to him that mummymummy had gone to be with Jesus.

The funeral was two days later, on Saturday. Lydia was never impressed by traditions, either she didn't know of them or she just brushed them aside. Her wish, her instruction, was that her coffin would not be brought into the church for her funeral. So we left it outside. Some of her family members were unsettled by this; we had overlooked that there was no opportunity for them to honour her by sharing the carrying of her coffin. This was remedied later, when they carried her body to the grave for burial. We were grateful for the way in which these family members honoured Lydia. They had loved her and they shared our sense of loss.

Gordon sat with us at the front of the church, not noticeably grief-stricken, but quiet and solemn. Our life-long friend, Fred Stephens, conducted the service. I spoke about my mother, a high privilege. I think my dad would have loved to do it, but either didn't feel up to the challenge, or – more likely – he chose to give it to me. At the burial ground we sang hymns of praise, we prayed, and Lydia's body was interred.

Now I had to explain to Gordon the two complementary truths about his mother's death. I told him that – as he knew – she had become very old and tired and she had lots of pains. So Jesus knew it was time for her to go to heaven. She didn't need her old body because Jesus made her a beautiful new one, and she would never be old and tired again. Because she belonged to Jesus, she would be properly well and happy always. That's why we put her old body into the ground.

Whether my theology helped Gordon I can't judge, but if you asked him 'where's mummy now?' he answered 'He'ben'. On the other hand if you drove past the graveyard, Gogo would point towards it with a casual thumb, 'Mummymummy'.

The people of the church had, while we were away, set out food, and we feasted and rejoiced. The woman who used to say she 'just chatted' with the Lord was in His presence. How could we sorrow?

Your God will be your glory.
Your sun will never set again,

and your moon will wane no more;
the Lord will be your everlasting light,
and your days of sorrow will end.

Isaiah 60:20

It was exactly one week after Abigail's wedding, and lots of wedding guests were with us at the funeral, and they had photos! There was no pall of gloom, it was a fine day, and we simply revelled in the love of friends and family. It was exactly the sort of function that was to Gordon's taste. Funerals never made him sad. There were mercies in his disability.

13

HE WHOSE WALK IS BLAMELESS

WILL and Gordon sorted out their lives together, free now from heavy concern for Lydia. My dad bought a simple cookery book, and set himself to produce good food for his son. I visited often, they visited our home, and every now and then, Will would phone me, saying, 'Would you be able to have Gogo for a few days? I'd like to go over to the West, or to England to visit [brother] Fred, or John and Helga, or Pat and Marion...' He simply loved to get away! He was able to do it now, and the freedom was like a tonic to him.

On one trip through Dublin Airport my dad got into conversation with a staff member at one of the counters, and the talk turned to the Gospel of Jesus. When Will learned that this lady had no Bible, he took her name. He bought a Bible before coming home, and after some difficulty in finding his friend, he gave her new Bible to her.

Gordon had an equally great time. The fears for his safety that Lydia had developed in her later years had been a bit stifling for him. When he was about to leave home to get the bus, she would say 'Gogey darling, be sure not to get off the bus in town. Just stay in it and then come back home.' Having an over-protective mother was just something a businessman had to suffer. He took no notice, of course. It was just mummymummy being herself. He came and went at his own pleasure.

I did get a couple of phone calls from a Greystones friend of my mother's, suggesting to me that my brother was being neglected;

his clothes and hair, sometimes his bristly chin, were not up to standard. It didn't bother me. The gallant fellow was healthy, happy, well fed and loved. What was the problem?

From the Sublime to the ... Dog. I wrote in my diary in July that year that our Springer Spaniel dog was 'simply crawling with fleas'! Gordon loved Springer, who was growing old, and he forgave him for an episode that was so ludicrous that in the fun of it all we overlooked Gogo's nearly having a heart attack. A beautiful, hot Summer's day in the garden. Keith was working hard, and in the heat he had taken off his shirt. After a bit of encouragement, Gogo did likewise. He was slightly embarrassed, but very proud of the semi-naked figure he cut, and he prepared to go up the garden to help Keith; two robust men doing men's work.

As Gordon turned his back on the shirt, Springer saw his chance. He shot over, snatched the shirt and tore up the long garden with his treasure billowing behind him like a spinnaker. Gordon nearly lost his mind, stampeding after the wicked dog, without a hope of catching him. His face flamed and he roared ''pringer! Bo' dog! Bo' dog!'

We got it back. Springer just wanted to have fun, to shake things up a bit; he meant no harm. Gordon stuffed himself back into his shirt, and I'm glad I didn't understand his growlings and mutterings. I would have been very shocked.

In October we had had some discussions with the Peacehaven people about a possible place for Gordon. He stayed with us for a fortnight, and during that time he actually had dinner and a sleepover in Peacehaven. I was sunk in depression and started to have medication at the beginning of 1993.

Springer became a very old dog, and started falling over. Our vet was waiting for us to decide when to have our pet's life mercifully ended. In July we phoned that we would bring him in. I phoned Keith to tell him and he said 'Don't take him yet. Wait until after dinner. I want to see him again'. As we were having dinner Virginia made Springer a little chicken sandwich and fed it to him under the table. Eventually Virginia and I slowly led him out to the car, and instead of turning left to be eased into it, he turned right to go for a walk!

But almost immediately he fell over, and we knew we were doing the right thing. In the vet's surgery Virginia hugged his front end and I hugged his back end, and he fell asleep.

We were let out like fugitives through the back door, lest we frighten the waiting clients by our tears. Keith, Abigail, and especially Virginia, whose dog he really was, were bewildered by grief, helplessly saying, 'I wish Springer could come back', heartbroken. Abigail sent us a card, 'sealed and stamped with tears'. As my tribute, I did his portrait in oils, and, in a frame on our living room wall he's sitting on fresh grass in the summer garden.

A little black and white toddler puppy had brightened and challenged Springer's last weeks. She was spayed, grew up and became the perfect dog. Posy was loved on sight by confirmed dog haters. She grew old after years of bringing us joy, and when she started helplessly walking round and round in ever tightening circles, we brought her to the vet, and her confusion was ended. This time it was Keith with me, and his heart was broken. Why, oh why do we do it?

I visited John and my sister Dorothy/Helga. They were so good to me. Will turned 87.

> Tell me who you live with, and I will tell you who you are.
>
> **Spanish Proverb**

Throughout 1993 we, Keith and I, had talked of buying a house which would accommodate us and my father and Gordon. Will would not be able to go on caring for his boy; what should be done? A house with a miraculous 'Papa & Gogo flat' would do. But we looked and looked. The nice ones were too expensive, and our purpose wouldn't be achieved by compromising.

We were wasting time. On 16th July 1994 we invited Will and Gordon to come to live with us. They moved five days later, fell into our hands like two ripe apples. Afterwards my dad told me that when he had done his shopping in Tesco in Greystones, he was often too tired to walk home, something over half a kilometre, downhill. He would sit on the wall and ask God to send someone with a car to give him a lift.

They had to share a room in our house, but they were great friends. Will planned to get a writing table to put in the window, having all sorts of plans to write letters, articles, notes on Bible study, now that he wasn't tied by domestic chores. But the pressure was off my dad, and he slowly began to crumble. He would come down to breakfast, late, after Keith and Gordon had left for work, wearing his fawn suit, looking tentative, with no particular plans for the day.

'It's a lovely day. Could we go out in the car, maybe to Marlay Park or St Enda's for a walk?' So we would. I dropped what I was doing, and off we went in the car on an expotition. If I had suggested that we might join Christopher Robin and Pooh Bear on their journey to the North Pole, Will would have been delighted. He always had a suppressed longing for adventure. But in the routines of the common round his grace, his deliberate contentment, were the marks of the man he was. Then he learned to use the TV.

He had never had anything to do with it, not from narrow-minded principle, more from lack of opportunity, and from a probable disdain for its frivolous content. He saw a couple of things on ours, became interested, learned to use the controls, and started to watch programmes. Two wearying factors were, first, his hearing was terrible, and if, like him, you haven't grown up listening to radio and TV, your ear isn't attuned to it. So he turned up the sound. After he had done that, and had unwittingly chased other people out of the room, hands over their ears, the second wearying step followed. He would ask me to explain to him whatever he was watching. Generally, he wasn't impressed.

We got a second TV for the sitting room at the back of the house, to which people could escape, and that is what they did.

The Old Man Coughs in the Night

Will started to cough. It was very troublesome, and I took him to our GP, several times. He went for x-rays to the Meath Hospital. At one of our visits to the doctor, my dad said that he was sorry for being such a nuisance. Dr David Gibney said carefully, 'Mr Cochran, you have never for one moment been a nuisance, since the first time you came to see me.' A brilliant doctor, and a very kind man.

Gordon had another weekend in Peacehaven. We appreciated that. One day he and I went to Belfast on the train. We had a great day out, taking in a lunchtime concert in Queen's University. At concerts he behaved beautifully, but there would be the little not-quite-noiseless hums and chuckles when he was surprised by pleasure.

At the end of October we brought Will and Gordon with us when we went away with our church for the annual long weekend, to The Cliff, a guest house in Tramore, Co. Waterford. Gogo loved it all, and took some trips into Waterford by bus, to lay his claim to new territory. Everybody accepted him, easily, with warm companionship. My dad was distressed by his cough, day and night.

Softly he wakes in the pre-dawn peace.
Fear creeps in, he waits.
He will not cough!
Gripping the blanket he lies still,
His body flares with heat.
The cough splits the night.

He said that he hid his head under the covers, not to disturb people.

Home again, my dad was visited by a nurse, Mary. He loved her to bits! He went to the Meath Hospital and to St James's to have ECG tests, and to see a geriatrician. He refused to let me drive him to St James's Hospital, insisting on using the patients' minibus service. The bus goes all over the place, for hours. He was exhausted.

Meals were challenging. My dad found many foods hard to get down. He asked me if I could make mashed potato a bit softer. 'I love mashed potato,' he told me.

On the twenty-second of November two Peacehaven Trustees came, miserably, to tell us that they had been advised that Gordon would never be able to adapt to life in the home. These two men were our friends, and it was a horrible thing they had to do. It wasn't their fault, nor was it a matter of their judgement. But at that time it was accepted as the right advice.

I started to research residential places for Gordon.

For some time I had had the support of a Home Help, Vivienne, who was employed by the Health Services. She prepared lunch for Will, and did the ironing for me, and made wonderful apple tarts, almost my dad's favourite food. I was able to go out for a while on those days. I wrote in my diary,

> Vivienne, a treasure.

On the ninth of December my dad was admitted to the Meath Hospital in the city, West Wing, D Ward. He refused to let us have him moved to a private room. His solicitor Philip Russell with great kindness travelled from Bray, Co. Wicklow, to visit him to sort out his concerns. I was there when Philip arrived, in torrential rain. The poor man had no umbrella. One of his small children had done something terrible to the only one he possessed.

During this time our hearts were lifted with joy! We had a family celebration. Virginia had been working on a doctoral thesis in Trinity College. On 21st December, she phoned me from town. 'I'm a Doctor!' she announced. She had defended her thesis successfully and was to be awarded a PhD with no further work, research or amendments required.

I visited my dad most days. Just before Christmas a nurse in the hospital told me that my father was doing very well, and might be allowed out for Christmas. I stood in front of her and started to cry. *I could not do it.*

He wasn't anywhere near being fit to come home. At Christmas he was photographed sitting on his bed, wearing a paper hat.

On the afternoon of the 8th January I went to see him. I wanted so much to give him something, and I asked what he would like. He said he wanted nothing.

'Take all that stuff home', he said, waving at the 'stuff' he had accumulated. 'Leave the Bible, *He's restoring my soul.*'

Abigail visited her Papa in hospital that evening. Early next morning Virginia heard the phone and woke me. The nurse told me that my father had passed away. In the context of recent months, my jubilant response to her was 'Oh, how wonderful! He's escaped!' Poor nurse, what could she say next? I calmed down then and made proper grown-up responses. Afterwards, I had a short explosion of tears, when my heart was overcome. The man had been my friend.

It was still very early. When Gordon came down for breakfast I told him that the most exciting thing had happened, that Daddy had gone to be with Jesus. He listened carefully, then picked up his briefcase, rolled umbrella and coat, and went off for the day.

Around mid-morning Keith and I set out to drive to the hospital to do the necessary practical things. We never had a notion as to where Gogo went during his day's work, but suddenly we saw him crossing the road. We pulled in, told him where we were going, and invited him to come.

The three of us went into the hallway of the hospital, and what followed was a positive orgy of handshaking and greeting. Gordon managed to combine mournful gravity with holy glee. Keith and

I did our best to act appropriately, but we were mere acolytes to my brother's High Priestly presence. Every hand that could be shaken was shaken – nurses, doctors, orderlies, delivery people, visitors and any ambulatory patients who were blessed by crossing our path.

'Gordon', I said firmly, 'Keith and I *(only us, please!)* are going with this nurse to collect Daddy's things, and to say goodbye to his body. We'll be back in a few minutes. You can sit here, and watch everything. Ok?'

Would I never learn?

Led by Gordon and the nurse, Keith and I walked down the corridor to the Mortuary, where we surveyed Will's body. Following what I believed was the principle of fixing in Gogo's mind the realisation that Dad's body was truly dead, I talked him through the evidence. Place hand on chilly forehead, feel toes which were, of course, sticking up... then Keith prayed. I would love to have heard the attendant nurse describing it to her friends that evening.

Clutching the hospital black plastic sack – almost empty because my dad had sent most of his stuff home the previous day – we left, thanking everybody in sight. Fewer handshakes, now, just lordly salutations, because the job was done, and there was the next thing to enjoy. Gordon suggested going for coffee, so we went to Rathmines, and sat upstairs in the Swan Centre, and felt very, very odd.

14

NOW, WHAT ABOUT GORDON?

AFTER we had coffee together in Rathmines, Gordon went to work. He needed to make the best use of the rest of his interrupted day. After dinner that evening, he went up to what was now his room and had a look around. He came down wearing Will's suit. He wore it every day till the fabric almost became transparent, then worked his way through the rest of the meagre wardrobe.

Mantled thus, did he feel like his dad? Was his dream being realised? Was he turning into his hero?

As expected, Gordon enjoyed Will's funeral very much, looking lovely in his dad's clothes. The service was in our church in Mount Merrion; Virginia spoke about her Papa. For Gordon there were so many people to greet! After the burial in Greystones we went back to the church. It didn't have pews, so while we were gone, professional caterers who were also our friends had filled the space with round tables. On each table was a centrepiece of yellow primroses nestled in ruffled blue napkins. We were served delicious food from a buffet. People caught up with family news, and Gordon was charmingly sociable.

Then, having eaten his fill, and getting bored and fed up with it all, he gathered up his briefcase, umbrella and coat, strode over to the door, turned, waved magisterially at the company and went back to work.

In December 1994, just before my father's death, I had written to the two senior office-holders on the Peacehaven committee, who had visited us unhappily the previous month.

> As we reflect on your visit, we appreciate that the staff would find Gordon challenging. We acknowledge the problems of his independent character, his poor hygiene, and his language difficulties. As far as speech is concerned, people learn quickly to understand him. He doesn't cover a wide range of topics.
>
> We would put it to you, especially being conscious of residents with whom Peacehaven has taken great pains, and also conscious of those residents who need, and receive, a high level of personal attention, that the following positive factors should be considered as part of the overall picture of Gordon.
>
> He is good-humoured and sociable.
>
> He has excellent health, takes no medication.
>
> He seems to have no sexual consciousness, never a whiff of a problem.
>
> He has no emotional or psychological turmoils, doesn't need counselling.
>
> He sleeps like a log.
>
> He can learn, as we've observed, new social and practical skills. Since living with us he has shown unexpected flexibility and willingness to learn.
>
> He understands everything that's said to him, and listens patiently.
>
> In view of the overall picture, while being aware of the undoubted disadvantage of his being handicapped, we believe that Gordon could be a manageable part of a group.

Four months later, on the 27th March 1995, I wrote on behalf of Keith and myself to the committee managing Peacehaven, copying it to each member individually. In it we regretted putting what might seem to be unfair pressure on them, but said that we believed the time was right for the 'Gordon question' to be addressed.

I listed our reasons for approaching them at that time. Gordon had accepted, and adapted to, many changes following the deaths of his parents. It would be to his advantage if the next, ideally permanent, change were to be effected without a long delay. Visiting Peacehaven for short periods would ease him in, and help to make a move natural and easy. The time was right for us. We had certain responsibilities to our family, which included ongoing support for long-term illness, giving support to several ageing relatives, to our church, and to each other. I was tired.

Also, I had no sibling or close family member on my side who could help.

I offered to step down from the committee, and to resign as a Trustee, if it would make the decision easier. In essence, our family must come first, with Gordon a very close second. It was imperative that we sorted out Gordon's long-term future as a matter of urgency.

Meanwhile, I met with Dr Vincent Molony, Director, and also Clinical Director, of the Mental Handicap Service of the Eastern Health Board, who worked from the Good Counsel Centre in Dublin 16, to talk again, and then again, about Gogo's future. He approached the Camphill Centre, at Duffcarraig in Co. Wexford.

David Dunne, working with the EHB Special Hospital Care Programme, took me through the complexities of the Disability Allowance system, with great patience, and ultimate success.

I had learned about L'Arche community, homes for people with intellectual disabilities. In 1964 the founder, Jean Vanier, began his lifetime involvement with people who had special needs by sharing his home with two disabled men. I attended an inspiring lecture he gave in UCD in Dublin. He was a philosopher and theologian who was moved by the 'cry for love' that he heard from such people, and he said simply that Jesus brought him to them. He had thought that he would do good to them, but they transformed his life.

Before any progress was made in pursuit of these options, some changes meant that Peacehaven began to look like a very possible future answer to Gordon's needs.

Meanwhile, Gordon had found a new friend. Michael Doyle, who was a volunteer with the Red Cross, came to us every week to take him out for a treat, for burgers in McDonalds maybe, and to supervise his bathing, to cut his toenails, and to be a sort of big brother. They had fun together. Michael's steadfast friendship was a blessing to Gordon, and we very much appreciated it.

In Peacehaven, as the committee prepared to appoint some new staff members, Richie Rowan, who was a member of the Board of Management, took over the management of the house. He invited me to meet him to talk about Gordon's situation. We met in the Avoca Handweavers cafe, at Kilmacanogue, and Richie came up with some ideas.

On February 7th Gordon went off to work as usual, and I met Richie again. I gave him an overnight bag packed with Gordon's things. In the evening by arrangement, instead of coming home, Gordon went to Greystones for a sleepover, and came back to us the next day.

Progress by degrees

Throughout the Spring of 1995, every few weeks Richie phoned and invited Gordon to visit Greystones. He began to accumulate a colossal mileage. Using public transport from our house to Peacehaven meant taking a bus into town and then a train or bus to Bray or Greystones, and then from the train either another bus journey or a longish walk. Going cross-country in the number 75 bus to Dun Laoghaire didn't appeal. Since the general idea for Gordon was to travel hopefully, it didn't matter how long it took. Arriving was the point at which he began to make plans for the next trip. In the end, always coming home, because as Margaret

Thatcher observed, 'Home is where you come to when you have nothing better to do.'

Our friend in church, Isabel, had a special relationship with Gordon. He knew her well. She loved and understood him. They relished a bit of fun, with plenty of happy banter. Gordon spent overnights with Izzy in February, and in March, and he was in his element.

Also in March Gordon took the bus into town, then the bus to Heuston station, and the train to Galway, then a Galway bus, to stay with Maggie Murray and her family and their dog, Rocky. Two days later he came home. Margaret spoke to me on the phone, telling me how the days had been spent.

> Friday: shopping, Taizé meeting. Saturday: market, Eason's for papers, Ideal Homes Exhibition (lots of leaflets), bath – scrubbed himself, Margaret washed his hair. Sunday: Mass, dinner, Ideal Homes again, train home.

She said that he's the perfect guest, more than welcome to come again, gorgeous with kids, he sang and talked lots, loved Rocky the dog, a credit to his family, he helped – got coal, cleared the table, tidied. Superb, no bother.

Spring 1995 rolled into Summer, and Richie kept in touch, inviting Gordon to sleep-over in Peacehaven. And Michael Doyle came and took him out for treats, and tidied up his nails, and saw that he was thoroughly bathed – a voluntary valet to Gordon the Gent. Michael, an absolute rock of kindness.

In June I met Richie again for a chat, and, on the strength of that, we booked a family holiday in Barbados! Gordon went to stay in Peacehaven while we were away, and off we flew. When we arrived home we found that Gordon had arrived back at our house far too early. He had been rescued by our neighbours Mick and Ann King who lived across across the road, when they saw him standing forlorn on our doorstep. They took him into their house and he settled happily, being treated like a lord, and fed with good things. I think our arrival was a bit premature for him, he was perfectly happy with his new friends.

In early July Gordon spent a whole week with Maggie Murray and her family. Wonderful Margaret, the dearest friend a Gogo could ever have. I visited John and Helga in England. In mid July Keith suddenly became very ill with acute diverticulitis, and was taken by ambulance to the Meath Hospital. For ten days he was unable to eat. Then the infection cleared up quite suddenly, and he was allowed to eat immediately! He came home at the beginning of August.

Not being inclined to idleness, while Keith was busy in hospital, Gordon and I went to see a chiropodist, who fixed up his knobbly toes. I'd better write about his feet now, because they've become relevant. At some stage, growing up, Gordon decided to wear two pairs of socks, at the same time. If two pairs are good – and it was so comfy – three or more pairs would be better, so by the time we visited the chiropodist he was putting several (four or five) on each foot, pulling them up tightly, and cramming his feet into shoes that were by this time much too small. It's only one of many Gogo aberrations from normal custom, but it was just the most ridiculous practice. Feebly, I wasn't able to stop him.

Keith, reduced to skin and bone, convalesced in the garden in the most beautiful warm sunshine, and recovered. Gordon socialised enthusiastically, heading back to Maggie Murray. He spent a day with another church friend, Mrs Pat Lundberg.

He visited Peacehaven, where he met a new staff member, Salome, who became a very dear friend. When Gordon and I had sessions of looking through magazines, he continued to be drawn very much to women in gowns, or more precisely to gowns on women, complemented by the enchantment of high-heeled shoes. It was a toss-up whether he would fantasise about me wearing the glad rags, or Salome.

HELLO! magazine was created for him, *OK!* is ok, but it's not the best. Gordon stabs at a page with a grubby finger, showing me a spectacular gown. 'Wow!' I'm winding him up, 'Yes it is a lovely dress, but, sorry Gogo, I don't think I'll wear it.' Gogo, thinking 'Ruth is such a dope', corrects me. 'Omey 'Omey!!' he tells me. 'Salome would wear it'. 'Nonsense,' I respond, 'it's for me! I'm your best beloved sister.'

Ok, little brother. It looks as if I have to share you. You've found another sister, best friend, and one who is just such good fun.

It was because of the newspapers that his hands were always piggy-dirty. They were rough and gnarled from being out in all weathers, and from carrying his heavy briefcase. Of course he had gloves, and of course he didn't wear them – they might get dirty. Newsprint gravitated lovingly onto Gordon's hands, even as he had gravitated lovingly to the papers in the first place, as they waited for him in the newsagent's shop.

It was the end of the summer, and Gogo went again to Maggie Murray.

My mother's sister, Essie, who lived in a retirement home, had hip surgery in the Adelaide Hospital in inner-city Dublin. As her nearest and possibly dearest, I was the one who managed her affairs. After our previous family illnesses it was so refreshing to have a change of hospital! After some time in the Adelaide, she was moved to the Orthopaedic Hospital in Clontarf. More refreshment!

She suffered a stroke, and was moved to Peamount Hospital at Newcastle, where I visited her. Not often enough, to judge by a comment made to me by one of her friends.

And then – in 1995, in the middle of September, a miracle. A room was prepared for Gordon in Peacehaven, and he was invited to go there to live. The steady kindness and wise judgment of Richie Rowan, all summer long, had been preparing Gordon for this.

Now, how was I going to tell Gordon? I had to get it right first time. I didn't want him appearing back to us from force of habit, nor for him to become disenchanted and decide that Rathfarnham pastures were greener. Peacehaven was to be his home, his base, his shelter, and the place where his heart would rest.

'Gordon,' I began brightly. 'You know how, when you go to Peacehaven, you have to take your pyjamas and your shaver and your briefcase and your papers and all your stuff with you? And when it's time to come back here, you've got to pack up all your stuff again and do that long journey, and it's so disappointing and such a bother?'

Yes, he agreed with all that. I ploughed on, 'Well, the best thing has happened! Peacehaven has a bedroom for you. It's going to be your very own room and you can keep all your things there, in the drawers and the wardrobe, and you'll never have to pack them all up and trudge back here. You can go to live in Peacehaven *all the time*, as soon as you like!'

Straightaway, my brother went to live in Peacehaven, and almost immediately started to call it 'ome.

I will tell of the kindnesses of the Lord,
The deeds for which He is to be praised,
according to all the Lord has done for us,
according to his compassion and many kindnesses.

Isaiah 63:7

Behaviour Modification

Peacehaven hosted a barbecue party, and I talked to one of the staff members, asking him how my brother was settling down. He smiled – everybody smiled when Gordon's name came up! Apart from some 'behaviour modification' everything was going swimmingly. A few of Gordon's foibles did need to be sorted out, nothing serious. He needed to learn to wear one sock on each foot, to come home for dinner in the late afternoon rather than the late evening, to eat fairly normal, mainstream food at mealtimes.

Lydia had taught Gordon all sorts of good things, and he had

Gordon cooks up a storm with sister Ruth in Blackheath Gardens.

Virginia, Lydia, Abigail, Will, Jeremy, Keith and Gordon in the garden of 124 Butterfield Park in Rathfarnham, Dublin.

'Tattins', special waitress in Bewley's, Grafton Street.

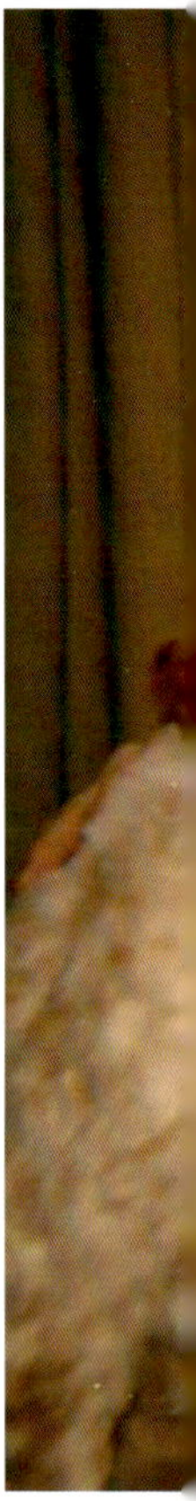

A dentist's dream, with Springer the dog, or a dentist's nightmare (*below*)!

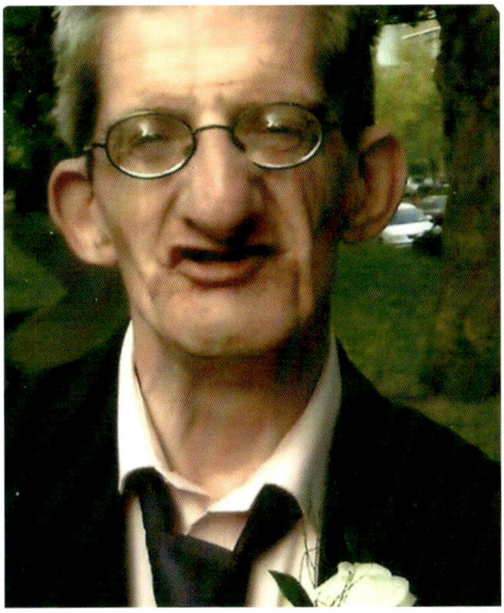

At Jeremy and Susie's wedding, aged 52.

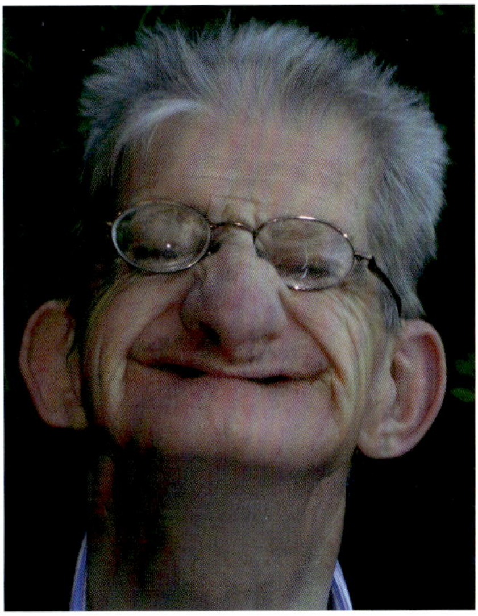

1

2

5

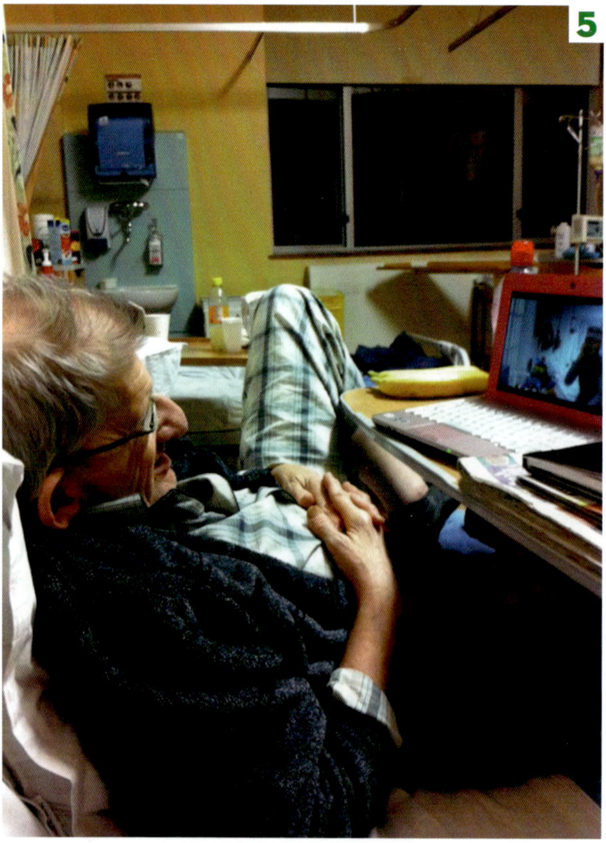

1. A man needs a good hydrangea.

2. *OK!*'s ok, but *HELLO!*'s better.

3. A very thoughtful gent.

4. Christmas Eve in Ruth's house. Many chuckles make light work.

5. You just have to try to relax in hospital.

6. Home again, in my special comfy chair, with a very odd newspaper!

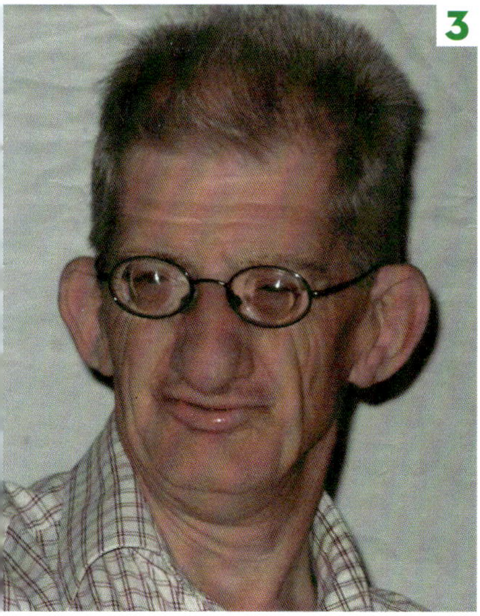
3

4

6

Training my thoughts on a trip to the Grand Canyon.

First check the timetable.

Arrested! They think I'm a spy!

America's not very safe – I'm going home!

The troubadours on tour in America in 2010.

My lovely friend! I was brave and Salome was delighted to see me.

Below: I don't go on trains any more. My friends take me to the station.

grown to be a gentleman. Being an independent sort of gent, and with his mother no longer trying – or able – to mould him, he dragged himself up the rest of the way, with mixed success.

At home with his parents, or with us, he wasn't always hungry at mealtimes, but after the meal was over, he would quickly feel a sandwich coming on. Into the fridge, and grabbing the sliced pan, the butter and the ham – or cheese if he'd eaten all the ham – he would put together a splendiferous creation, bursting with filling. With a fat sandwich, Gordon was a sound trencherman. Over time, in Peacehaven, he grew to enjoy proper meals, and to eat food he had never met at his parents' table. On his birthdays, when he could choose the dinner-party menu, he reverted to traditional tastes and his choice was turkey (or chicken) and ham, with all the trimmings, with jelly and cream for pudding.

A bread-based snack needs a drink. With the weekly groceries, Lydia always bought a bottle of Orange Squash, which Gogo loved. Very smartly she would hide it away, so that it could be doled out in moderate amounts. The next day, when Gordon was having a sandwich, she would go to get the squash, to give him a treat, and then the careful plotting would come to grief. She couldn't remember where she'd hidden it. Frustrated, she would say, 'Gogo, I can't find the squash. I can't remember where I put it.' Her helpful boy would put down his sambo, go and take the bottle from its hiding place and give it to his mother.

I didn't see the sock issue being dealt with, but it was. He wears beautiful shoes, and his feet slip smoothly into them.

His bedroom. His bed. Oh how very odd is my lovely brother! In Clontarf, and then with his parents in Greystones, Gordon's bedroom was his den. I'll explain. There was a chest of drawers. In one drawer was a dense jumble of socks; in those days he needed a lot of socks. The next drawer held newspapers and magazines, evidence of a rich collection, curated by a connoisseur. Regrettably, even though at first Gogo might have treasured a newspaper or a mag, when he was done with it, he always tore it in half. Then it went into the drawer, and when the drawer was packed, and couldn't be closed, into the bin.

He did that with papers and magazines that he stole, too. Infuriating. I would go to sneak a look at his room, and in the waste basket would be my latest House & Garden, torn in half. When he cherished really special things, they went behind his pillows. Sometimes there were rich pickings. I found a French magazine. He must have been puzzled by it, because the pages consisted only of meaningless coloured designs. I knew what to do. Looking at one of the pages, I let my eyes relax, and with altered focus, I could see, in three scandalous dimensions, a very saucy image. And another one in every page. Well, so I assume. The magazine was wasted on Gordon, he would never have been able to see the pictures, he was protected from them, *and I am glad he was.* Nevertheless, in my head I can hear his chuckle, 'Ho-ho! Bo' man! Bo' lady!'

Another drawer in Gordon's chest held a pandemonium of broken umbrellas. Sometimes they broke because he was a bit rough with them; sometimes he got fed up with the current one; sometimes the new one, gleaned as he tidied up the train or bus, was so lovely that he discarded the old one forthwith. If he was near home, he stashed it in his room – he had briefly been fond of it – otherwise it went into a public bin.

Back to his bed. At the head, he arranged an empty space. The pillow was placed well down, to where a man's shoulders would be, because when Gordon went to bed, part of the preliminaries was to lay his briefcase, his umbrella and his papers above the pillow. Then he snuggled in, very cosy, except that his feet generously overhung the end.

When he came to us, he would remake his perfectly fine bed, prepared with love by his big sister. In the cupboard were spare blankets, quilts and pillows, and he took most of them. He stripped the bed, put about half of the bedding in a layer onto the mattress (a prince, afraid a pea might keep him awake), then a sheet, then everything else layered over that. In this nest he would sleep like a dormouse, his head invisible, and his feet in all their pallid beauty sticking out the other end.

Gordon grew to love life in Peacehaven. He and the other residents developed deep affection for each other, marred sometimes by fierce and bitter quarrels. War broke out when Gordon thought he had the supreme right to sit in the front seat in the car, but somebody else believed he had that privilege as well. Gordon never suggested 'I would like to do this or that'. He managed to indicate that the entitlement to sit in front was his from birth, and there was to be no discussion.

The other entitlement he claimed was to take the day's post off the hall table and distribute it. He, document man, was of all people eligible to do it. There was more war; somebody else loved doing that job. Henceforth no resident was allowed to touch the post.

15

THE SIMPLE UNCLE

A FRIEND of one of our children said one day 'I saw your simple uncle'. Hmmm ... there were two other uncles, but we were confident that she meant Gordon.

'Simple', a kindly adjective, had many years ago replaced 'Innocent', which had been a general term used to refer to people who were simple-minded, slow-witted, idiots – a blanket term used in the psychiatric dark ages. It was assumed that Innocent people were free from moral wrong, a charming fantasy, as these individuals were by no means innocent. As research and understanding advanced new descriptive terms were coined. A Mentally Handicapped person, whose whole identity carried the label, in time became a child or adult who had an Intellectual Disability, which is a fierce mouthful, but accurate. It showed the changed understanding, that the person was not defined by his disability. He was a regular man or woman who had a problem and who needed support. He is now a person who has Special Needs. The beauty of this is that people can support each other, each using his strength to meet the need of another.

While I was making this book, I emailed Gordon's nieces and nephew with questions, asking for insights into life with Gordon, from their perspectives as children and teenagers. Following are extracts from Virginia's reply to my questions.

> First question: certainly not, ever, scary/uncouth/pathetic, and I did not consider (when I was a child) that Gordon

might have been a 'frightful burden' to Nana and Papa, although I knew he took Papa's papers and Nana's clothes, and I heard that he hit her, which I found hard to believe but assumed was from frustration. I did not know about many of the practicalities of managing him for Nana and Papa.

One thing I remember her describing to me: the morning of your wedding, Nana hanging out Gogo's sheets on the line (he still wet the bed, aged 10) and her crying into the sheets as she hung them. It was so helpful that Nana was open about things. None of it worried me, because I didn't feel as if things to do with Gordon were being hidden from me.

I was aware how much Nana adored him, and couldn't enjoy any treat if 'Gogey' was missing it. Nana had learned about his condition, and how to help him, with speech therapy etc, and all done by public transport. She seemed devoted to him, and I did not think that a bad thing. Some people need a person to be devoted to them.

I saw her influence in his gentle, affable manner, making friends wherever he went. I was always happy to be with him – he was fun! In small doses. He had a great sense of humour, and it was so rewarding to make jokes with him. I invited Gordon to my 21st birthday party (the one for my friends, rather than the lunch for elderly relations the next day) because he was part of my life. I valued him as much as anyone else at my party. Different, yes, but so what?

Letting Gordon travel alone was brave of his parents, and was the right decision on the whole. One time there was a family party at Abigail & Ciaran's house, and he was determined to go under his own steam. He got lost, and people went out to look for him, and a kind stranger took him into his car and drove him round. When they eventually met with one of the family, Ciaran I think, the man was critical, saying that Gordon should not have been let wander around alone.

I did find Gordon noisy, but he had to be, being surrounded by so much deafness. It was nobody's fault that his hands were always excessively dirty. We all tried to get him to wash them properly!

After Gordon had moved in to live with you and Dad, David and I stayed overnight at Christmas. Our room was beside Gordon's and he was against the radiator, which banged every time he moved. We crept into his room and pulled the bed away from the heater, with him in it, and he slept right through.

In church he sang very loudly and attended to his socks but I can't recall any disruptive behaviour. Sighing deeply during long sermons I regarded as an appropriate reaction.

I never felt any awkwardness about Gordon being around my friends, and I never questioned his place in the family or his purpose: he just was. Easy for me, because I knew him always, and he had a place in the family before I did. I didn't even wonder about the God question, when I was a child and growing up. Does a person have to be for something? Now, as an adult, I know and accept that there's no earthly answer to the God question.

Life's Rich Pageant

What, knocked a tooth out? Never mind dear, laugh it off, laugh it off; it's all part of life's rich pageant.

Arthur Marshall

A tooth abscess and extraction was my next adventure, and this became literally a cry for help, a shriek of anguish. Our doctor came in the evening to fix me with painkilling drugs, then later in the night we summoned a Doctor on Call. He came and gave me more medication for pain, and to sort out the side effects of the first lot. A couple of days later I recovered, tired but happy.

With Gordon happily settled into Peacehaven, we went on holiday to Glengariff and Kinsale, places which are beautiful beyond description. After that I had a bout of reactive depression.

I visited a counsellor, a Gestalt therapist. It was interesting, and I would have enjoyed very much having her as a friend, but being continually told to 'breathe' rattled me. Anyway, I could have written the script. I was too cynical and ironic to take it seriously. A psychiatrist in St Patrick's Hospital was kind, and seeing him was restful, particularly as he contentedly sucked his pipe during our sessions.

I had been, after my father died, engaged in a great deal of correspondence with the Peacehaven Trustees, and during the ensuing months with different departments within the (then) Eastern Health Board. The disability benefit which Gordon was receiving was, at that time, the Disabled Person's Maintenance Allowance, and I needed it to be made available to Peacehaven, as the charity had become Gordon's agent in my place. I also claimed a lunch subsidy for him – explaining why he didn't get 'free' lunch. The people who attended workshops were given lunch. We had to find somewhere for Gordon to have lunch, and to pay for it, during his day in town. This was an extra expense, for which the EHB didn't normally allow.

The manager of the Footprints café, in Talbot Street, agreed to give Gordon coffee and a sandwich at lunchtime, and to send Peacehaven monthly bills. In an exquisite coincidence, the manager of the café, which was attached to the Scripture Union Bookshop, was Elva Byrne, from Blessington, a daughter of my mother's childhood friend, Gladys.

I estimated with the Health Board what discretionary living

expenses Gordon might need on top of the basic Disability Allowance and lunch funding, such as clothes, small gifts, social outlay, perhaps a holiday, which would otherwise be covered by a wage from a workshop. All Gordon's records with the Health Board needed to be changed, and it was complicated by his having moved from Greystones to Rathfarnham, and now back again.

When Gordon went to live in Peacehaven, I wrote to Salome, telling her his life story to date, details of family, friends, health, daily habits, idiosyncrasies, food, personal hygiene, lack of same, obsessions, daily 'work'. I told her what we knew of the mysteries of his travelling, which at that time wasn't very much.

Later we learned that his travels extended to Malahide, Howth, Dublin Airport, Kilcoole, Kildare. I told Salome of his joy when the buses and trains were 'acked' full to bursting, how he would write down his notion of the number of cars blocking up the streets; at first it was 160, then it grew to 260!

It strikes me now that Gordon genuinely loves numbers and figures. He learned to write words, but the focus, the reason for the words, was the accompanying number. Bus numbers, house, telephone, age, date, timetable, hymn, page, Bible chapter numbers; numbers are clear and precise, immutable. You could trust a number, hold on to it.

> I like mathematics. It's a beautiful subject that allows you to express so many things. Numerical answers can be correct with an absoluteness that words do not have. I sometimes write computer code, where there is an elegance and simplicity to a right answer – and if the code looks inelegant, then the method is probably inelegant too. There's a rightness about mathematics that you don't always get in language.

These are the words of Dr Stuart Neilson, mathematician and

computer scientist, who would surely be a man after my brother's own heart. Words were tricky, hard to write, and there were far too many of them. Even seasoned wordsmiths have problems with the tools they love to use.

Words strain, Crack and sometimes break, under the burden, Under the tension, slip, slide, perish, Decay with imprecision, will not stay in place, will not stay still.

When T.S Eliot wrote that, he may have been utterly exasperated, at the end of his poetic tether. Far too many words. I wish Gordon could have known that a celebrated poet shared his frustration. I wish he could have revelled in discussing maths with Dr Neilson, one of his own kind.

The trains were always very 'ong, with 20 carriages, and hauled by 'hooge' engines. Hooge would have indicated really a large size or number, though Gogo hasn't a notion about thousands or millions, or about kilograms or millimetres, ounces or miles. If we had had the wit to see all this, could we have had fun together playing with numbers? We could have used mealtimes, with crockery and cutlery.

'Gogo, you have a coffee cup, and here's another one, and there are two more. Do you know how many we have? Can you say it?'

'Yes, perfect! Two cups of coffee, one for you, one for me, then two more cups, one for daddydaddy and one for Keith; we're four people, four cups.'

'How many biscuits would you like, one or two? Ha! Ok, you can have two, both of them, and Dad can have the other two. Keith and I will have... none!'

He was comfortable with two, and used it. We could have had happy times exploring three and four and ten! His dad was enthralled with maths. It simply never occurred to us that Gordon might have had an aptitude. He did enjoy music, very much, and rhythm. Music and maths – I knew from Enid Blyton's 'Irene', in Malory Towers, that the two went together.

In telling Salome about Gogo's life, I detailed his dental history, chiropody, dates of forthcoming visits to us, past events, free travel pass, very poor sight, conservative taste in clothes (a passion for French cuffs and cufflinks), taste in music. I warned her that, because he had been badly burned years ago, he would need effective sun protection. I told her about Gogo's pleasure in copying out A4 sized pages and pages of bus and train timetables, and about his annual Railway World subscription.

I described to Salome his rejection of new ideas, and how I dealt with that – get his attention, go into confrontation calmly, knowing that your will is strong. He panics when he's rushed or confused. I told her that Gordon doesn't know how to sulk, and that after a battle of wills he's immediately your friend again, that he loves to be praised, and that he's demonstrative, delighting to give and receive hugs.

The fact that, starting from scratch in Peacehaven, he wouldn't be able to tell anybody anything, was in my mind all the time. I wanted to make life as easy as possible for the staff, and for Gordon.

Progress was all right; only it went on too long.

James Thurber, attrib

I debated, by letter with Dr Vincent Molony, the question of Gordon's being made a Ward of Court, and with our solicitor Philip Russell whether Peacehaven could be absolved from responsibility for Gordon when he was out travelling. That arose because all the other people who were intellectually disabled, going to and from workshop, were thought apparently to be under some sort of remote supervision.

It went on and on, and I did become a bit tetchy, as in an early letter to one of the EHB's officers.

> DPMA – Gordon Cochran 26th January 1995.
> (note spelling of Gordon's surname)
> Dear Ms -
> I enclose the completed pink form re the above, and thank you for your help.
> I do want to make the point that the third section is completely irrelevant. If anybody needs a medical opinion it is I. Gordon's disability has been clearly established, and has never been in question. His eligibility for the DPMA is not at issue here.

The person, or people, who were dealing with Gordon's case persistently misspelt his surname, giving it a terminal e, which displeased me.

In another letter, I went past tetchy,

> DPMA – Gordon Cochran 1st May 1996
> Dear Mr -,
> I enclose completed DPMA Review form. Please note the spelling of Gordon's surname.
> You will see that on 24th October 1995 I notified your office ... subsequently I had confirmation from Mr ..., and also by Ms ..., that Gordon is still eligible for the allowance ...
> You will appreciate my exasperation at the ridiculous delay – a short scan through Gordon's file would have made the matter clear, and saved your office, as well as myself, a good deal of time and trouble.

In July, Mrs Doyle, of the Rathfarnham Post Office, was helpful in clarifying the DPMA payment protocols. I spoke to an officer of the Wicklow EHB. A new DPMA book was being prepared, and it would be sent to Peacehaven. It would show the new agent to be Geoffrey Hanan, Trustee, representing the charity.

The envelopes addressed to Gordon from the DPMA would arrive in Peacehaven, and I warned the staff members that, no matter how persuasive he was, Gordon was not to be allowed to touch them! They were for Geoffrey, and for him alone.

In an explanatory letter to Geoffrey, I finished,

> I hope everything runs as planned now.

From Gordon's point of view, everything was running swimmingly! My diary documented my helter-skelter lifestyle, while my dear brother's life was simply happy. He came, by arrangement, to visit us often and always went – a happy homing pigeon – straight back, by arrangement, to Peacehaven. From the first day of his new life, that was never a problem.

He often visited Margaret/Maggie in Galway, had wonderful times, led Maggie a merry dance, and went home.

My busy days kept me from missing Gordon too much. We had people to stay; I was helping to support my mother-in-law, and my aunt, in their old age; my diary tells me that I had 'fierce gastric flu'; we had work done on the house (my dad had told me that we should get the kitchen refurbished!), I was involved with the Peacehaven Board, and in our church. I qualified to teach adult literacy, and taught for a year. Every now and then I met Gordon in the Footprints café for lunch. We went on holiday to Crete, and I went to visit Dorothy/Helga and her partner John in the South of England. Gordon came to us at Christmas, of course, and has done so every year until 2012, when he stayed at home. At the beginning of 1997 I felt a bit tired and wrote dramatically, Such Difficult Days!

Happy Days

In March 1997 Virginia and David announced their engagement. That was a Very Happy Day.

In June the whole Peacehaven household, with some privileged family and friends, was invited to visit President Mary Robinson in Áras an Uachtaráin. She mingled with us and chatted with everybody and we had afternoon tea, and pretty well invaded the Áras, and we all glowed with pride and excitement. I suppose every single person in the party understood who Mrs Robinson was, except Gordon. But he didn't know that he didn't know! He also glowed, because there was such a rarefied atmosphere and we were all dressed up (to impress the President?), and there was an extra grace and polish to our collective demeanour and conversation.

On August 28th Abigail and Ciaran were blessed with their first child. Chloe Lydia was, as you would expect, adorable, exquisite, clever - well, that didn't show then, but of course she would be clever - and our collective happiness couldn't be measured.

On October 18th David and Virginia were married, on a day of shining sun. Abigail was her sister's attendant, and in Abigail's arms the Flower Baby slept. She was seven weeks old, she had a tiny posy of flowers on her dress, and she was as quiet as a mouse.

Helga/Dorothy and John came over for the wedding, and they stayed in a Guest House in Greystones. Gordon was, of course, a guest, and it was planned that they would come to the church from Greystones with Gordon, sharing a taxi. So the trio set off towards Dublin.

'Can you take us to South Hill Evangelical Church?' asked John. The taxi driver, baffled, queried 'What's the *name* of the church?' He was hoping that a familiar Saint's name would put him right. 'That is the name, it's in Mount Merrion somewhere.' John was getting flustered. Aware that time was passing, he turned to Gordon, 'Gordon, can you help us, d'you know where the church is?' Gordon knew where everything was. He took over, and he guided the driver, and they arrived in good time.

Adventures for Gordon had been fairly modest, sedentary affairs, compared with the activities of other ordinary people, sportsmen, travellers, climbers, swimmers. Will's and Lydia's adventures had been mostly of the mind and of the spirit, with occasional trips by train or in a car to visit people and to visit places close by. Belfast/Aho had always been a place worth visiting.

Adventure for Peacehaven residents was on a different scale. It didn't involve a very long journey, but at journey's end the thrills and fun began, and Gordon was in a new world. Peacehaven went every year to a week's camp at Ovoca Manor Adventure Centre, in County Wicklow. The holiday centre belongs to Scripture Union, and to entertain the people who stay there the activities include death-defying and nerve-jangling challenges, too many for any single adventurer to try out, or for me to list. The terrifying ones include a Zip Line, the Leap of Faith – just looking at the online pictures makes me want to hide underneath the table. Canoeing and mountain walks are less scary, and Bushcraft and Orienteering sound reassuringly manageable, as though they were designed to keep one safe. Youth Groups, school children, teens and adults, families, groups of all sorts are challenged, they make friends and have fun, and they hear what God says to them through the Bible.

Peacehaven's week at Ovoca is the All Ability Camp. The place is full of people from near and far who need some form of support, and there's a full complement of volunteers. I suspect that for people with disabilities, a week at Ovoca simply transforms them.

Ovoca has always been a great adventure. However, there came a day when 'Adventure', for the Peacehaven people, was comprehensively redefined.

America

Denise

Belfast

84

BELLE THE DOG

INSURANCE

Seán

HUGEMAN

TO GOD BE THE GLORY

Rocky the dog

RTE Lyric

Phil and Betty

Ham sandwiches

TEA WITH THE STATIONMASTER

16

I SING BECAUSE I'M HAPPY!

And singing still dost soar, and soaring ever singest.

Shelley, To a Skylark

WHEN Gordon went to live in Peacehaven, I knew that he might not quite fit in. I didn't know what could be done about it. He was extremely un-mouldable, as his mother discovered, and as later I experienced. He was a man of decided tastes and deep-rooted inherited characteristics. His all-embracing friendliness, his brotherhood with everybody in his world, the instinct to help people – did those attributes come from his mother? The probability of a clever brain, though disabled by injury, and his distinctive comportment – from his father?

His need to sing at the most unsuitable times, in the most unsuitable places, in the early morning when his house-mates need to sleep, in bathrooms, public and private; where that came from I don't know, but I've got it too. Gordon and I share it. It's got a name; it's called earworming. It's being earnestly researched by academics. There are continuous melodies going through the mind, looping and meandering on and on and on, and it's impossible not to sing, or hum, or, in my case to whistle because I can no longer sing. I do try to control when and where I do it, but Gordon just lets it all out. When his spirit soars, he sings.

When he went to live in Peacehaven, I wrote to the staff, giving them my permission – which was presumptuous, they didn't need permission from me, because Gordon was an adult – and more properly, giving them my blessing, to do whatever they felt was good for Gordon, to help him to adapt and to make it easy for his new housemates.

But I said, 'Do not break his spirit.'

They didn't. *His spirit soared.*

A soaring spirit is an adventure in joy.

A very different adventure, of physically soaring, introduces new joys.

In 1999 a group of Peacehaven residents, which included Gordon, with staff and volunteers – one companion for each resident – gathered at Dublin Airport. They checked in their luggage, and they felt that particular excitement that says, 'No going back now!' When the time came, they boarded the plane and found their seats. The doors were slammed shut, the pilot welcomed them, cabin staff checked that everything was in order, the engines, which had been purring, alarmingly thundered, and the plane suddenly started scorching along the runway. They were pressed back into their seats, and then the nose lifted, they climbed the empty air, the ground streamed away, the engine calmed down, and they were soaring!

For hours they hovered in the sky while the world rolled away underneath them. Then the plane floated down and they landed with a little bump near Paris. The Peacehaven Group were booked into Disneyland. They had a wonderful, spectacular, overwhelming, fun-filled holiday.

Salome, the Peacehaven Holiday Wizard, had researched, chosen, arranged and booked everything. The holiday was fairly easy to plan, not much of a challenge to a holiday wizard. Paris is lovely. But it's only in the near bit of Europe, and now they'd been there and done that. Other Disney locations, in the USA, for example, began to beckon. Salome, undaunted, undauntable, called on her own travel experiences, and the Peacehaven people started to invade the United States.

They did it in 2003. Again, in 2007 they did it, going to San Diego, and to a resort in California. In front of me are the details of a visit they made in March 2010, to two different locations. The full printed itinerary takes six A4 pages. Every flight number and time, destination, every website, phone and fax number, email address, the online booking references, accommodation addresses, all details of insurance, every vehicle that was rented, every contact name, is recorded in this priceless document. Eight residents travelled, with eight people supporting them; five of these were staff members, one was a close friend and two staff members' spouses made up the assistants. Two of the residents were wheelchair users, another one had impaired sight, and one had impaired speech and hearing.

In brief, they flew to Atlanta, then on to Tucson, Arizona, where they stayed in a hotel and rented two Dodge vans. During that week the party went to Studios where Westerns were filmed, to an air base, to an All-American State Fair Ostrich Festival with rides and shows, to church, to an overnight in Williams, and a shoot-out, followed by the steam train trip of a lifetime into the Grand Canyon. Back in Tucson, they visited Tombstone, famous for the OK Corral and Wyatt Earp, where they saw a re-enactment of the famous 1800s shoot-out. On one trip the train was held up by 'train robbers', collecting tips. Gordon was held at gunpoint on the train, which he thought was hilarious. For the second week they flew to Orlando, Florida.

They rented two more Dodge vans and settled into two villas. That was Disney week. It included riding roller-coasters, petting dolphins, meeting Disney characters, rides, a visit to Epcot, to the World showcase, to a flower and garden Festival. On the Sundays, they took time over their daily devotions, and the holidaymakers chose songs and readings, and they led prayers. Then out and about again. They went to The Animal Kingdom, on Safari, to a Character Dinner, back to Sea World, and then the long journey home. Fifteen people, and my kid brother.

I would mention two things. All these trips were funded by the residents, from their own savings, and from gifts and fund-raising specifically for the trip; the Peacehaven resources were not plundered. Also, I referred to daily devotions. As important as air and food to the group were the morning times set aside to read the Bible and to pray, to thank God for His protection and provision for them, and to ask Him to bless the activities of the day.

17

IRELAND'S NOT BAD, EITHER - ESPECIALLY AT CHRISTMAS!

PEACEHAVEN established two special Christmas traditions.

The first one was a sensational Christmas Dinner Party which was held about ten days before the Day itself. Staff members, residents from the different houses, Board members, family members... about fifty people feasted in the big dining room, packed with tables, and decorated with lights. The food was wonderful, the complete Christmas Dinner. It takes a long time to finish feasting; there are crackers to pull, funny hats to put on and jokes to read out, and then there are speeches.

The residents love making speeches, some people speak with eloquence, and some are less eloquent, but our hearts are always touched, and there's lots of gentle teasing and laughter. One young woman has speaking and hearing disabilities, but that's not a problem. She uses sign language and some staff members can sign, so we heard her speech interpreted in somebody else's voice. Gordon loves making speeches, of course. Anything you can do... So he took the floor, and in bursts of communication, waving the arm in emphasis, he thanked everybody in sight for coming, thanked the people who cooked, thanked any odds and bods who caught his eye, and was encouraged to sit down. Well satisfied, he eventually did. Salome, who is the house manager, can read his mind as if his head were transparent, and she interpreted for him.

After that, we packed into one of the sitting rooms, Salome sat at the piano to play for us, and we sang almost every carol in the book, no two of the unique voices matching. There is almost nothing to touch the sheer joy of it all, nor to equal the difficulty of singing with a lump in the throat.

The other memorable event was the Pantomime! Still feeling very festive and in party mood, early in January all the Peacehaven people, together with invited friends and relations, met in what was then the Dome restaurant at the top of the St Stephen's Green Centre in Dublin. Tables were laid ready for us, and we had dinner together. We were only a step across the road from the Gaiety Theatre, and, well fed and fortified, we made our way to the front rows which were reserved for us. The lights went down and the fun started! The people in the very front row were almost in the orchestra pit, and the musicians, for that evening, became our friends.

Nobody puts on Birthday Parties like Peacehaven! The happy celebrant chooses the menu. I've only been to Gordon's birthdays, so I don't know what other residents choose to eat. Gogo doesn't have exotic tastes, and for him, if Christmas dinner is a good thing, have it as often as possible. Which is why on every September 27th we sit down in Peacehaven to Christmas Dinner, to celebrate Gordon.

It takes a while to eat our way through it, and we chatter and have second helpings, and it's eventually finished. The guests would probably include Salome's parents, Fred and Ruth, whom Gordon adores, and railway-man Brendan and his wife Pauline, Seán from Blake House, perhaps Kingsley Prescott, who has been a good friend and a companion on special junkets. But the evening hasn't reached its climax. In Peacehaven the birthday man or woman doesn't touch a single birthday present until dinner's finished. They've all been saved up for this moment. Gordon opens parcels with no finesse. The most beautiful, carefully chosen wrapping papers and labels and ribbons are wrenched open, torn to flitters and cast away, and we behold the gift. Then it's passed from person to person round the table, with each guest commenting on its beauty, quality and usefulness, till it goes back to the star of the show. There might be ten or a dozen presents, so this can go on a bit, especially as the guests get over-excited and the comments become colourful. Eventually, Gordon has the fun of gathering up and crumpling the sea of torn paper and stuffing it into bags for disposal. He's likely to disappear at this point. His presents often include something to wear, a crisp shirt or a tie, even a woolly jumper, so up in his room he delightedly takes off the old and puts on the new, and shyly presents himself to his guests, who applaud his beauty. Then if guests have a shred of energy left, we all go into the sitting room and Salome plays piano and we sing hymns!

Having lots of birthday cards is gratifying, and getting presents is great fun, but Gordon has had another birthday tribute. Can any of my readers match this most splendid one? Is it unique to Gordon? My brother-in-law Stuart had just left Bray, travelling South on the Rosslare train. He was enjoying the peaceful journey. Suddenly the peace was broken. A very Official Voice came over the intercom, filling the train. 'May I have your attention please? On behalf of the staff of Irish Rail, we would like to wish Gordon a Very Happy Birthday!' The outburst of clapping nearly broke the windows.

Someone had the bright notion of giving Gogo a Filofax. Every week he enjoyed copying the staff rota into its pages. It took a long time, but it was the sort of work that suited him, detailed, exact, and pre-eminently useful. Having that back-up was a comfort for the staff, to know that whatever distracted them, Gordon was keeping things steady. Could we say that my brother worked part-time in Admin? *Pro bono*, of course.

Another family party appeared on the horizon! Our son Jeremy and beautiful Susie announced their engagement, and on 28th May 2005 they were married in our church. Susie's family and friends came from Germany, and there were guests from Belgium and Scotland and England. After the service we had cake and wine in the church. Gordon discovered that he *loved* Prosecco, and he became very happy! Mingling among the guests, he hugged everybody in sight, quite blissed-out, ignored by his big sister who should have kept an eye on him. Later, fifty-five of us, including Gordon of course, had dinner on a barge as it drifted up, then down, the Grand Canal, and there were speeches and music and dancing. At midnight on the top deck, we, including Gordon, ended the celebrations in a forest of waving sparklers.

Give Thanks with a Grateful Heart

Gordon tended to go to bed quite early – well, people in Peacehaven Admin don't generally need to work late into the evening. It meant that he was well rested by morning. The down-side for the household was that for Gogo morning started before seven. As my brother washed (I can't guarantee that he washed, though he enjoyed baths), and put on his lovely clothes, full of the joy of the Lord, he happily and endlessly sang. He gave thanks with a grateful heart. His house-mates did not.

In fact, several times when I've been at a Peacehaven party, one of the gentlemen who shared the house with Gordon took me aside, saying 'Can I speak to you later? I want to talk – about Gordon'. My heart sinking, I said, 'Yes, of course, we'll make a time to talk'.

Later, I would be cornered. 'Now, what's the problem?' I'd ask, knowing perfectly well what was bothering my friend. A grave face gazed at me, small steady eyes fixed sombrely on mine. 'Gordon sings. Early. He wakes me up. Will you tell him to stop?'

I said I would. I said that I *perfectly* understood this man's problem; Gordon used to do it when he lived with us, so I know what it's like. My friend has my complete sympathy. Yes I would of course speak with Gordon.

As, during the next couple of years, Gordon's days were very much changed, that particular problem solved itself.

Gogo's life was bound up in the Peacehaven world, but it also had its own rhythm, and that continued. He visited Maggie

Murray, more usually known as Margaret Donohue, his almost life-long friend. He had made the journey time after time to her home in Galway, with no problems. He was 57, beginning to get on a bit. Because he had no teeth his face was small, and his hair, always trendily cut short, had gone from dark brown, to grey, to silvery, to sparse.

The staff at Peacehaven helped him to buy beautiful clothes, in keeping with his self-image as the polished smartly-dressed CEO of ... what company? The companies he knew about had been part of his life in Dublin. He had learned of them through conversations with his mother in the streets as they visited them or passed them, and she later showed him the names in phone books and in newspapers.

Gordon's business aspirations would stretch to Booley's, 'Lery's, EBS, Bank, 'surance. He wasn't out early enough in the day to witness the great morning rush of people going to these places, but in the evening when they poured out onto the streets, Gordon was there. As they raced for trains and buses they didn't even notice one of the happiest men in Dublin who walked with them, striding along swinging his briefcase, and whose life was, at that moment, completely fulfilled.

While I was a Director of Peacehaven, and at the same time Gordon's closest family member – not his mother, as some people have supposed me to be – I received monthly reports from Salome, his house manager, and sometimes from Denise, who is his keyworker. Those reports are a diary of Gogo's life, written about him of course, not by him.

In the course of telling my brother's life story, I've included some extracts from my mother's diary, and I have imagined what my sister Dorothy might have written in her diary, and I've quoted from my own. Now I'm going to rummage around in my brother's monthly diaries, written by his carers, and pick my way through a few years. I've used Gordon's voice to tell his stories, from his own point of view. Most of the material is taken, with small adjustments, from the monthly reports. In telling the story of Gordon, of every event, of every small detail of his days, I've told the simple documented truth.

18

GORDON SPEAKS

We are a Garden wall'd around,
chosen and made a unique Ground;
A little Spot inclos'd by Grace out of the World's wide Wilderness.

Isaac Watts

2009. March. I visited Maggie in Galway. I waited at the station, and Maggie found me at 10 pm. They're a bit over-protective. Talking about getting me a special mobile phone with only two numbers, for emergencies. What emergencies?

Brendan is coming to visit me. He's my friend, a railway man. In the Coffee Shop in Connolly Station they're my friends too. I usually have a fried breakfast there. I had a great time at Camp and ate loads!

April. I hear that they've got a better plan for me than a two-number phone. That's good, I was a bit embarrassed by the whole idea. What sort of man uses a phone with only two numbers! They want to get one with GPS. I don't know much about that, but I'm told they could use it to find out where I am. Peter's looking after this. I'm feeling pretty Special!

A speech therapist is visiting me. I had one visiting me years ago when I was just a boy, I think mum got her. Do I need one? I manage ok. I find that people are a bit slow. I'm going to get a Communications Passport. Denise is finding and laminating some pictures that I can show to people.

I wanted to go on a church day away, but on the morning I needed to stay in bed with a sore tummy and couldn't go. I got up after a while and I felt very well.

May. Sometimes I do unexpected things. And I like to help people. I went to the doctor's surgery to save trouble, but the people at home thought they were going to bring me. The doctor didn't seem know what I was there for. I remember standing Ruth up one morning, because I had to go somewhere else first, but I got to the NCH in time for the concert, so everything was ok. Well, she seemed a bit peeved for a few minutes. Moody, maybe. Women!

Chores are a burden. They make me so weary, and people never stop reminding me. My ironing is getting better! I go to the weekly Bible Study, lots of my friends are there, and at Easter I went to Messiah in Greystones. 'Hallelujah' wasn't quite up to standard, but I had a great time. My friends in the butcher's shop offered me a job, and I laughed my head off. A job as a butcher! What would my dad think of that?

June. I love going for evening walks, but they told me that it would be better if I walked instead of getting the bus down to the station and back again. That's silly, the bus is quicker. I'm told I have high cholesterol, and I need my cataracts checked, and we got some wider shoes for me as my feet were squashed. I voted on polling day. They explained 'voting'. We could do that in Peacehaven to change things. I do try to change some silly ideas people have.

August. The GPS is working. I've been given a new Iarnród Éireann shirt by my Railway friends at the station. The people here at home found a kitchen knife under my pillow again. I use it to poke about in my shaver, to fix it. DIY is good, I like fixing things, I don't want to be looking for help all the time. They said (again) that I can't keep a knife in my room. Fusspots.

I am SO excited to be going to America next year. I'm up early in the mornings and I read out the list of helpers and residents who are coming with me. I've been asked to tone my excitement down while other people are still asleep.

September. For my birthday I got tickets for a Steam Train Trip from Connolly to Mullingar.

October. I visited Maggie and helped her to sort out her newspapers. My friends at home are going through my Personal Outcome Measures with me. I've to set some goals and talk about my life. Not sure about goals, I think it's a wish-list. I have lots of wishes. At the bag-pack in Dunnes, fund-raising for the holiday, they said I was a fantastic help. The check-out lady got on very well with me, and said I did a brilliant job. I love helping people.

November. I love Strictly Come Dancing. They told me not to put dirty pots away with the clean ones, I have to wash them first. They didn't look very dirty to me. Sometimes I can't make up my mind about going out, and then when I come down with my coat and my Bible it's too late.

December. I can't wait for Christmas to begin. There's a new Arrow train. We loved doing Christmas shopping in Dundrum Town Centre; dinner in TGIs reminded me of America! My Personal Outcomes thing is called POM, which is not a proper word. People should use the proper words. I said that I feel sad sometimes. We think I'm missing my mum and dad; when they went to live with Jesus they left me behind.

> I do feel sad inside sometimes, it makes me feel very tired, and sort of old. My people here at Peacehaven do love me and they help me with hard things, and I feel safe here. One of my POMs is to Look Over my Basic Human Rights. That'll be interesting.

Here I'm intruding into Gordon's Diary. When I met with his care staff, that is Denise (Gordon's keyworker), Salome (house manager) and Vivienne (Company Manager) for an Annual Review, I heard mostly happy positives. He has strong affection for his housemates; he chooses to attend a Wednesday prayer meeting at the church, which he very much enjoys. Other people at that meeting can now understand a lot more of what he's saying. Gordon baths every day and splashes to his heart's content. Some of his top priorities were, to sort out his sad feelings regarding his parents; to go to Belfast with Denise and another staff member, Peter; to meet and talk with two housemates about their treating him unfairly; to go to the National Concert Hall. His GPS device is a huge help, it's padlocked onto his trousers. When he fails to meet people – as happened with Maggie Murray – he can be traced. It's a fabulous gadget; using Google Earth, it transmits Gogo's coordinates to the computer, and then he can be caught!

> December 2009, January 2010. Before the Christmas Dinner in my house I put out all the hymnbooks for carol singing. I made a speech welcoming everybody, I sang a duet with Fred (Salome's father, a best friend). I went carol-singing with his Bible study group. I went with Salome's family and friends for Christmas Eve breakfast in Dublin (oh, I love that, we do it every year), and Salome dropped me off at Ruth & Keith's to spend Christmas with them.
>
> Sally, who's one of my staff here, brought her parents to see me. They live in America, which is nice. I know

America, and it's lovely. I was able to show Sally's father all my train books. He's good on train stuff. I haven't seen many American trains, but Sally's dad told me that they're hooge!

I had fun at Disney on Ice. On New Year's Eve I went with people down to the pub and got a great reception from them all. I watched the New Year's Day Concert from Vienna. I got stuck for ages in Greystones station, the snow and ice were terrible, and I knew I'd crash down if I tried to move. The GPS was away being mended! They found me after I'd waited a long time, and it was so great to be safe home. The snow and ice kept me at home for a week. I was fed up. They even stopped the buses from going over Bray Head.

I went to the opticians again, though it had been only a year since my last visit. Salome felt that my eyesight was making life hard for me. The new optician in Greystones was great. My prescription was quite wrong. How did that happen? I answered all the questions perfectly, I could see all the silly things they showed me quite well. I'm to get new glasses. I really hope they'll work much better for me. I get a bit tired with things looking fuzzy.

When I'm getting ready for my bath, sometimes I have to peep out the door to see if anybody's waiting to get in, and I open the door forgetting that I haven't a stitch on! Oops! They want me to stop doing this. More fuss-potting. I get travel books from holiday shops to study while I'm waiting for the big holiday on the 10th March. I'm feeling great these days and enjoying all the food we get here.

February. It's less than 4 weeks to the big trip. You can imagine how excited we all are. It's so slow coming. We went bowling. I'm keen on bowling. I have my own style, which works very well. I made a short speech thanking everyone for coming. I was very unhappy about getting the swine flu injection. Two times I wouldn't get out of bed for the appointments. I got it the third time, but only after we were all worn out talking about it. Some of the guys in the house have been feeling sick, so I visited them in their rooms to cheer them up.

I'm not great with electric shavers, so one of the staff gives me a Wet Shave every couple of days. Brilliant, all men should have somebody to do this for them. No hassle at all. Denise went with me to get some new clothes, as some of my suits were getting raggy.

March. The Big Holiday – words fail me.

April/May. I visited the doctor and got some creams for the cracked skin on my hands.

(I, Ruth, have found that the skin on my hands has become allergic to newsprint. I haven't known anybody else afflicted in this way, but it seems that I share it with my kid brother.)

The doctor wants to investigate my heart murmur, so I'm waiting for an appointment. I heard them saying that murmurs can be serious in an older person. A murmur? I'm expecting them to tell me to keep quiet! (I think that's a joke. I've just made a joke!) At the Peacehaven Celebration I sang a beautiful duet with Fred. I was so happy to see Michael Doyle, my friend from Rathfarnham. We had a good chat together.

I visited my best friend Maggie, but we got a bit muddled about the time she expected me. Because I had my GPS with me (padlocked onto me, mortifying), the people at home were able to see where I was and tell Maggie. Maggie was very understanding and gracious about it, she was so delighted to see me.

I simply hate it when Salome's away, and sometimes in the night I start to cry. It's a lonely feeling. But daylight improves things, and then I'm in fine spirits. Next week I'm going to drive to Aho (Belfast to you) with Denise and Peter.

June. I went to the Moody Chorale concert in the Nazarene church – brilliant, and to the Greystones Orchestra 20th Anniversary Concert in the Holy Rosary Church. I have a programme from that with all the beautiful long words on it. I went with a couple of people to see my parents' graves. I do get very sad at night, and I can't help crying. In Aho we went on an open-top bus tour of the city. It was a great day. I love Denise's mum and dad, I call them Michelle and Wilf.

July. Isaac's Deli where I've been getting lunch in Dublin is closing, and the manager came to Greystones to tell me. I wished her success with her new coffee shop. It'll be quite close to Greystones. Denise and I discussed where I should get my lunch now, and I suggested the café in Connolly Station. We will go to see it on Saturday, and introduce ourselves to the staff. I'll bring money each day to buy lunch. I had a great week in Ovoca with my friends Kingsley, Fred and Seán Kelly. Great guys.

I seem to have stopped crying these days, that's a relief. Pesky chores. I get them done as quickly as possible, and then someone's not pleased because maybe I missed something.

> A sheltered life can be a daring life as well.
> For all serious daring starts from within.
>
> **Eudora Welty**

August. Chores again! Do they not know there's more to life than chores? Somehow the business of chores makes us argue. Well, they argue, I just let it flow over me. Now and again I do have to stand up for myself. But they're great people, and they love to help me. They made me a Picture Aid to use when ordering my lunch in the Connolly station café. It attaches to a key ring, and I do like it. It helps. There are other good places for me to get my lunch, and I suit myself about where I go, Bray, Greystones or Dublin. I've gone off eating dinners in the evening. We went swimming and I really enjoyed being in the water. I comforted my friend Seán when his mum died. I was able to be sad with him.

A wedding! I love weddings, especially the clothes. I love the special suits some of the men wear, and flowers in the buttonholes. I like to wear a flower as often as I can, you feel special. I remember I had a great time at Abigail's wedding, and then at Virginia's. And Jeremy's one was fun, with people speaking German all over the place (that's what I was told it was, sounded like rubbish to me), and a party on a boat!

I had another flower, a real beauty, for this other wedding I went to. Peter, one of the staff here got married, and of course I was included. The women at weddings look beautiful with posh dresses and high heels. Women need lots of high heels, I know my big sister loves high heels too. But I think you can't do chores in them. Back to pesky chores!

September. They say I'm very bossy... I'm excited about my birthday. In the mornings in bed or in the bath I'm thinking out loud about lists of the guests and the menu. Not about tidying or cleaning! You can tidy or clean anytime. They're a bit persistent about that. It's great having money in my pocket when I'm out in the mornings. It's meant for lunch, but once I hit the paper shop, well, I buy papers. I don't seem very hungry these days. We had a great battle in the house recently. One of the guys was reading the Radio Times, but I needed it just then, so I swiped it. He was quite upset, and we fought hard for it. Then it was in absolute ribbons, no good to him or to me. A pity.

October. The cold evenings are coming in and we're getting ready for winter. I'm happy these days, and being quite kind to people. And oh, I had such fun the other day! I like a full bath, but I forgot that when I get in the water comes up higher. I wonder why it does that? It spilled out over the edge! They've asked me to be more careful and of course I will. It just took me by surprise. The water has been seeping downstairs into the bathroom down there, and I think that's a bad thing. I had another happy visit to Maggie.

November. I'm not happy. I feel all mixed up and cross and sad, and I hate doing what I'm asked to do. I feel scared too, I don't know why. They would like me to get out of bed in the mornings, and it makes me cry, and I really have to fight them to leave me alone. I love Salome being with me, and I love Denise as well. I get a bit cross with Salome, but I don't mean to be cross with her. Denise spent time with me talking about it.

I went swimming. One of the guys had a tussle with me over a shirt we both thought we owned. I hit him in the face with a newspaper. Immediately, I said I was sorry. Well, I saw that it wasn't my shirt. A good thing shirts don't shred like the Radio Times. I told them that I didn't want to go on the church weekend away, but on the day before it I felt much better and said I would go after all. They said I couldn't. Salome explained that there wasn't enough time to arrange for a staff member to go with me. I was dreadfully upset and disappointed, and I cried a lot over the weekend.

December 2010 and January 2011. I have no appetite. The doctor gave me medicine and took blood tests. Yes, I do hate being poked with that needle, it's a mean thing to do to a man who's trying to be good. One day I had an idea! I told it to Sally, and we went to Insomnia in Greystones for coffee when we were shopping for a new umbrella (that's another story – had I run out of umbrellas?) Since then, people often saw me in Insomnia having a coffee and a cheese sandwich!

I was completely terrified of the snow and ice, and basically stayed indoors for the whole time. The staff suggested I might help around the house by doing some hoovering. They're quick enough to take advantage of a guy. I went to a wedding, and the bridesmaids had a simply HOOGE car. When the weather's good I like going to the Bible Study, I meet my friends there. I went to Messiah in Greystones, and Denise came with me to the NCH performance, the big one. I love the NCH, it's sometimes PACKED. Denise and I talked about what things I'd like to do next year, and we made a list. We'll start doing things in January. I love having lots of things to look forward to.

I don't go to work so early these days, I'm tired sometimes, and I don't feel well in town. Then I come home early. What age are businessmen when they retire? I feel a bit old, and I need to go to the lallo (you'd say loo) in the night, like old men do. Sometimes I make a bit of a puddle. They said I should put the light on. That was a great idea.

February. A few problems. I love visiting Fred & Ruth's house, because they're Salome's mum and dad. I like them a lot. They're my kind of people. Sometimes I borrow things from their house. They've told me not to do that. So I said sorry. As well, I like helping Vivienne and Lily in the office, and I empty the bin. Sometimes there are interesting-looking papers, so I take them to keep in my briefcase – well, they are rubbish, aren't they? Now I find that Lily is shredding all her papers, some new office procedure they've got.

I have to have cream put on my head! It gets a bit sore, and I suppose other people don't like the look of it. I do like to give my hair a really good scrub in the bath. I was planning to go to an important funeral a while ago, the lady who died was called Miss Blake. She's a great friend of my sister's. I knew her too. She would make you feel safe. I didn't feel like going on the day, so I stayed on in bed.

I visited Maggie again. I've decided I'd rather get a later train, with the businessmen. I had a wonderful time in Galway. Maggie says she likes my company.

I've gone off going to work. I'm fed up having to get up in the mornings. Town doesn't seem the same, it worries me. What would happen if I lay down in the street? It's comfortable at home. One of the people in the house is at home all day because they got hurt, so there's a staff person here, and I don't need to get up and out. Anyway, we had one of those little chats and I said I'd get up and ready for the day by 10 o'clock. If it makes them happy then I'm happy. They're bothered by sore places on my head. I try to clean them off, but they don't go away.

March. I'm helping to get Sunday dinner ready, on Saturday evening. I'm peeling carrots. I love having visitors for lunch. The doctor says my blood's not ok, so another poke in two months. There was a terrible earthquake on the TV, and a huge wave from the sea in Japan. It was terrible. It made me feel terrible, watching it.

More trouble. Chores will be the death of me. I put fresh sheets on my bed when they tell me, but it seems

I need to take the old one off first. It looked fine the way I did it. People need to let up a bit. At the doctor again. She seemed pleased with me but I've to have MORE blood tests. Nobody seems to be poked as often as I do. They're not pleased with my blood. They're all so fussy. My blood doesn't bother me. Maybe some of the staff need pokes too, that would take their attention off me. I've discovered I love cooking, and I do the vegetables – well, some of them – for Sunday dinners. Carrots and potatoes are my speciality.

April. Last month I went to the Dublin St Patrick's Day Parade. Town was PACKED. Much better than Greystones. The dad of one of my friends in Peacehaven died. I was sad for him and I comforted him with lots of long hugs. I talked a good bit about my own mum and dad dying. My blood is better! I've to drink more water (boring), and eat good meals. Actually, I prefer Coke.

I was looking at papers in the office to see if there were any spare ones, but I was ticked off. Another chat. Then they got upset that I sometimes pee on the bathroom floor. It just happens, I feel all tangled up inside and tight and worried about something, and I can't really concentrate on doing a pee properly. Salome was off sick, and I don't feel so safe here when that happens. I'm used to her being here. I mostly don't do that pee flood when she's back at work.

May. Now I have plasters on my head! The embarrassment! I got new shoes, and trousers and some shirts. One of them's for best, so I like to wear it mostly. I only go to work for a couple of hours on some days now, semi-retired, I suppose. The women who are in the house with me are going to America, for a girls' holiday, so I'll go to Maggie.

19

TWO PARTIES, AND A PARTING

AFTER the first Peacehaven house was finished, and the residents and staff were settled, we began to plan for a second house. In due time we bought a beauty, and it was refurbished and adapted for its new purpose. It too was in Greystones, and we re-named it Blake House, to honour Miss Blake. She never accepted this, insisting that the name was in memory of her parents. Then after spending time, years, waiting and praying and thinking, we bought a third, again in Greystones. This one was to be a home for people who would live more independently, so it needed to be adapted for that purpose.

When all was ready, we had a party. Everybody, residents, staff, families and board members met in the house, in Applewood Heights, to look it over, and eat dessert and chatter. Gordon chose not to go. Several residents made speeches. One of the residents, a pretty, very young woman, stood up. Speech-making would have been difficult for her, so she sang. I had never heard anything like it. It was a random melody, sung quite naturally in the rich voice of a trained thirty-year-old, with a shimmering vibrato that caught our hearts.

For some years I had regularly called to the apartment in Sandycove where Miss Blake lived with her sister, to collect my friend and bring her to Greystones to committee meetings. After the two ladies moved to live in retirement in Our Lady's Manor in Dalkey, I picked her up there. By that time, the Peacehaven Trust had become a limited company, so we were directors.

Peacehaven was preparing for another party, and Miss Blake was feeling the burden of increasing age. She had never willingly submitted to being old. Many years previously her sister, Dr Lois Blake, took me aside one day, when my friend would have been about 75, and said severely to me, 'Have you any idea how old my sister is? She's doing far too much.'

The forthcoming party was for Peacehaven's Thirtieth Birthday, and it was a Celebration on a Grand Scale. The Nazarene Community Church in Greystones allowed us to use their spacious building, and we had a huge crowd of families, friends, friends of friends, residents, staff and our many supporters. Vivienne, who was Company Manager at the time, had brought in lots of flowers, and as part of the celebration she made a glamorous Birthday cake. Everybody who had any interest in, or was linked in any way to the Company, travelled to be with us. We sang and we prayed. There were speeches and accounts of the beginning of the charity, and its growth. Residents sang and spoke to us, they led individually in prayer. The resident who had no speech spoke to us, through a staff member. Gordon sang a duet with his great friend Fred. A number of the parents of residents spoke about what Peacehaven meant to them. Geoffrey Hanan, Financial Director spoke, I spoke, and Miss Blake spoke. A power-point presentation showed a stream of comments from residents and staff and others. The comments were made anonymously; they're moving and funny, and they tell the inside story of Peacehaven's people through intimate revelations. There was plenty of food, and the Birthday Cake.

Miss Blake was very frail, and she was brave. Courage, they say, is to keep going on even when one is terrified. We never doubted that she would come to the celebration and tell the story of Peacehaven. I wonder if in her heart of hearts she had qualms.

That morning when she was praying did she say, 'Heavenly Father, if I stand up, will you keep me standing? If I open my mouth, will you give me words? If I falter will you steady me? I have a little joke to tell. Will you help me to pull it off? I want to honour you and tell the truth.'

She had invested heart, mind, spirit, time and energy in Peacehaven. To some extent its story was her story. We asked some friends to bring her to the venue, and a little table with a lacy cloth was placed beside her chair at one end of the front row, with fresh water for her, as she had requested. (She had even offered to bring a glass to save us trouble.) On the morning of the event, having carefully chosen the spring-like clothes she wanted to wear for this literally once-in-a-lifetime celebration, she dressed herself. A member of the Nursing Home's staff came in to check whether she needed help, and told Miss Blake that her chosen outfit was unsuitable, impractical, too warm, too cold, or some such nonsense. My friend arrived wearing her old but good tweed suit, disappointed and struggling with anger. She had been victimised by some kindly-intentioned bullying, and I was appalled. A woman of this lady's age and personal stature should be allowed – allowed? – to make a frivolous choice. She was not senile. All her clothes were of beautiful quality, she was elegant in mind and appearance. At ninety-eight Miss Blake was entitled to choose for herself what she would wear.

A giant of courage, putting disappointment behind her, she rose to the occasion, stood up and delivered a masterly address, with clarity and yes, with wit.

Not long after that, I stood beside my friend. 'My dear' she said,' I'm sorry that you have to see me like this.'

Softly, Miss Blake spoke to me from her bed. Just short of her ninety-ninth birthday, she had been taken to hospital, and when I visited her it was clear that she was very near to the end of her life on earth. A Sister from the nursing home came to visit, and we talked gently for a while, then I prayed with my friend, and I kissed her and said goodbye and left the room, bereft. In the passageway, my eyes spilled. I was selfishly thinking only of my loss, the loss of my role model, my encourager, my inspiration, my friend, whose faith in God was as steady as granite and as soft as love.

Miss Blake's funeral was held on Monday 31st January 2011, in her church, Dun Laoghaire Evangelical Church. The people who came from Peacehaven sat in the front seats, except for Gordon, who stayed in bed.

A church elder led the service. Geoffrey spoke and I spoke.

'Can I go up to the front?' One of the Peacehaven residents came to me before the service with his request. This gentleman, a man of personal dignity, went to the front and stood beside the closed coffin that held our friend's body. He rested his hand on it and bowed his head. Later at the graveside he asked if he could pray, and everybody stood quietly while this man overrode his disability and praised and thanked God for the life of Miss Blake. This was an experience of death and grieving being transmuted into joy. It was a perfect moment.

'Now my dear, I won't be seeing you for a time.' In the middle of these emotional days I remembered the occasion, about twenty years previously, when Miss Blake made this announcement to me. 'I'll let you know when I expect to be with you all again, and then perhaps you'll be kind enough to collect me as usual.'

I was very concerned, it sounded worrying. Was she ill, was an operation looming? How brave she was! I didn't enquire, of course, one just didn't. There was such reticence, such fortitude. Miss Blake would tell us just what we needed to know, at the right time.

A few weeks later, she did. I got a postcard from some exotic spot in South America. Miss Dorothy Blake and Dr Lois Blake were on a world cruise.

Upstairs in a cupboard in my house are the diaries of the unforgettable journey, which Miss Blake gave to me to keep.

I will turn their mourning into gladness;
I will give them comfort and joy instead of sorrow.

Jeremiah

By June 2011 Gordon had stopped going out to work, and the

staff were providing twenty-four hour cover every day. Denise phoned me to bring me up to date. After that there were some things I wanted to say, for the record, so I wrote to Denise, Gordon's keyworker, for the staff, and to the Company Manager, Lily King, for the Board of Directors. I went over the points that Denise and I had covered, saying,

> I understand... the staff have to use every possible skill in managing Gordon without physical confrontation or overt bullying. I think that at times they must have been exhausted and discouraged... I appreciate the willingness of the local GP and the Heart Clinic staff to try to manage Gordon's illness while he stays at home.
>
> That's the situation regarding his health.
>
> His well-being is another matter. For 17 years I've observed Gordon at home in Peacehaven, and I know quite well that he's a complicated fellow, an opinionated sort of man, very obstinate and obsessive. I know that he's deeply loving, generous, caring about his fellow residents, and that he can be absolutely exasperating. He sings beautifully, but at inappropriate times.
>
> When he went to live in Peacehaven Gordon needed some 'behaviour modification', as a then staff member put it to me. I made only one proviso, that his spirit wouldn't be broken. Broken! Gordon's spirit has soared! The seventeen years have been pure blessing. Gordon has been soaked in steady love and clear guidance, and truckloads of celebrations and fun, and in this place he has matured into a most gracious gentleman.
>
> Now the purpose of all this is quite serious, which is why I'm writing. The time will come when Gordon's heart fails. It would be a joy if God were to take him quickly into His presence, but there may be a period of illness, or a sudden crisis when quick decisions would

need to be made. I'm not only referring to the medical situation, but to Gordon's dread of hospital and the effect an emergency admission would have on his spirit. None of us wants him to be frightened... to death.

I want to say that if such a crisis should arise, I absolutely trust my brother's carers to make the necessary decisions for his good. I give them that freedom, knowing that he could not be in wiser hands. I won't challenge the choices they may make. I will wholeheartedly support them, should there be questioning or critical voices.

If I'm available, of course I'll be part of the decision-making; the above is for a time when I might not be at the end of a phone.

I'm fully conscious that the other residents in the Peacehaven houses share the life that Gordon does, and they too are most blessed.

Time to go

On 27th June 2011, I resigned from the Board. It was time to do this, and not in any way connected with Gordon's poor health. I assumed that when I retired I'd be terribly sad and regretful, after more than thirty years with these people who were all my friends. In fact, I left my last meeting lightheartedly, clutching the flowers and things I'd been given, feeling only relief. The work had become specialised, the administration increasingly complicated. Though I had a certain amount of common-sense, I couldn't serve as an equal with the highly qualified staff and the board members who contributed their own professional experience and skills. I knew that I had shot my bolt, and Peacehaven was in the hands of superb people, and safe in the care of a superb God. I was free!

Difficult days

At the beginning of September it was my birthday, and Gordon didn't come. I forgave him, and on the 27th we went to his birthday party in Peacehaven. There were twenty-five people there to celebrate, friends and residents, staff members from other houses. We had lovely food – the September Christmas Dinner. We sang and there were speeches. Then Jonathan, one of his fellow residents, stood up and said 'Now we should pray for Gordon.' And that's what he did, he prayed for my brother on his birthday, reminding the Lord how they all loved him.

Denise spoke to me on the phone in mid-November. The staff were using prescribed sedation to help Gordon over difficult periods, but they didn't want the essential Gordon to be smothered by medication. They were working to devise a different life-style that would help to make him happy, without any pressures. He was refusing to carry things, such as water jugs in the kitchen, a shopping bag in Dunnes. His eyesight was deteriorating. He suddenly became anxious in the supermarket, shouting for Denise, in blind panic. His bed was his safe place. His physical health seemed to be reasonably good, cholesterol just being slightly raised.

The staff were taking courses to qualify in Non-Violent Crisis Intervention. Denise has done a course on the problems of adults with learning disabilities who self-harm.

Gordon's anxiety culminated in panic attacks, when his body let him down, adding embarrassment to his distress.

Denise emailed me on 23rd November 2011.

> Gordon has not had a good few weeks lately, and has been staying in bed till 6 pm some days. On some days I resort to helping him to dress and holding his arm to bring him downstairs just in an effort to help him be part of normal life in Peacehaven. Margaret offered to have Gordon come to Galway to stay for a little holiday but he declined.
>
> I took Gordon to the opticians on Monday afternoon. He did not manage to get there for the lunchtime

> appointment that was planned. It was very stressful for Gordon but the optician managed to get a reading of his eyesight and it seems that it has significantly changed and it is worse. Also he has some retinal degenerative disorder that is causing him problems. This is untreatable. We are waiting for the HSE to approve funding for new glasses. Making return visits is causing him anxiety.

During these weeks Gordon often chose to stay in bed all day, knocking on the floor or walls to get staff attention if he needed company. That is guaranteed to test a carer's patience, it's particularly irritating. There were many phone conversations, as Gordon's carers, doctors, psychologist, struggled to find out what was troubling him. Random comments from the staff, usually Denise, were,

> We want to give him choices... to take baby steps, not pushing him, he reacts by shoving... being able to choose, he's more content... depression?... some weeks of prescribed medication may help... he went out with Denise and Peter... he's self-harming, picking at his skin... he saw a psychiatrist... med was stopped, Denise is not keen on using a lot of med... at times Gordon seems almost manic, talking more, loudly... he refuses to attend medical appointments, even accompanied... maybe agoraphobia? ...he needs a colonoscopy, wouldn't leave the house; they'll do bloods instead... says Ow! when he's touched... we will take a holistic attitude – allow him to be heard, to lead the way.

I recalled the long period of depression he had suffered years previously, when 'work' became too stressful for him, and that his recovery began when he was given freedom.

The guiding principle was agreed, between the staff and the Board of Management, to Handle with Care. The other residents and the staff are a constant comfort to Gordon. He loves them.

Maggie Murray sent us a note with her Christmas card.

> I have been speaking with Gordon, and I was sorry that he wasn't able to visit us in Galway – we miss him and his lovely ways. Hopefully he will get over this and be on his merry way again. CIE minus Gordon just does not seem right! Everyone who knows him in Galway is hoping that he is on the road soon again. Time and love will hopefully restore his spirits.

On Christmas Eve Gordon was brought to us in Rathfarnham. That was a minor miracle of benevolent despotism. The Peacehaven houses had always been closed for Christmas, the residents scattering to their families and friends. On the assumption that 2011 would be no different, the rota had been fixed in advance to allow staff to make their personal plans. On arrival to us Gordon settled into his bedroom, giving me his medication to store in the fridge, and he seemed happy to be with us. He went to bed early, and I prepared for the next day, when our family would join us.

Keith went off early to the Christmas Morning Service at our church, as he was leading the service. I went to help Gordon to get up, planning to bring him in my car. He traditionally adored this day, and our church was full of his long-time friends, so there would be handshakes and hugs *go leor*, and beaming faces, and Gordon's voice swelling in joyful song. Of course he would never sit with me. Not when there were friends to sit beside.

He was buried in his bed. I started cheerfully to wake him up for this happy day. He hid himself deeper. I pulled the covers back a bit, gently. He curled up like a little caterpillar. When I encouraged him to get up he told me that he had a cold, he had a pain, he was sick... and he started to cry. He was my little brother, the soft baby whom

I had loved to cuddle when I was twelve. Now I was terrorising this worn-out middle-aged man. It took me half an hour to support him in getting up, by reasoning, enticing, making silly little jokes, suggesting, being firm and just loving him as hard as I could.

He came down and wouldn't eat breakfast. Briefly, oh so casually, I suggested what fun it would be to just drive down into the church garden, put our heads in through the doorway and wave, and then come straight home. Fun? No! What a dreadful idea! We stayed at home, we listened to beautiful music and we were comfortable. Then the extended family came, we feasted and exchanged presents, Gordon gathered up the wrappings in a black sack for recycling. He went to bed early, and the next morning we prepared to take him home.

He was happy, full of beans, all packed up, but he started to ask me something, and he kept on asking, and I couldn't understand him. We worked at it so hard, and he thought I was as thick as a plank. I felt irredeemably thick; there were no clues to help me. Gordon was being so patient with my stupidity. He was orally stymied. Then by some miracle I got it – his medicines were still in the fridge!

He had been a bit of a lost soul in our house. He slipped smoothly back into his safe slot in Greystones, where he was at peace.

> God, who comforts us... so that we can
> comfort those in any trouble.
>
> **Paul, to the Corinthians**

Gordon was in trouble. He would not eat. On the 6th January 2012 he was admitted to St Columcille's Hospital in Loughlinstown. He had been vomiting, his heartbeat was 170 beats per minute, and irregular. His heart wasn't functioning properly, it was enlarged, he was acutely constipated. He was at risk of cardiac arrest, and he had a lung infection. Denise was with him. She, and each staff member who was with him in turn, exhaustively explained everything to him, the tests, nursing procedures, strange noises.

She texted me:

It looks like he may be staying the night. His heart rate is taking time to even out. However, Gordon would rather go home. He won't lie on the bed and relax. He keeps looking at his watch and saying he wants to go home for tea.
Even though he hasn't eaten in a week!

I could sympathise with Denise! That hospital had witnessed Gordon in this mode many years ago, and at least one person who was present at that time has never forgotten.

It was decided that Gordon would stay for a couple of days, and he would be heavily sedated at night. It would give him respite, and the Peacehaven staff need not be with him for those sleeping hours. A staff member would stay beside him during all the rest of the time – which extended to 1.30 am on the first night because he couldn't go to sleep. Denise was told that some time after going home, he would be called back to hospital for more tests. After speaking on the phone with Lily King, I emailed her and the staff, putting on record the substance of our conversation.

> I agree that Gordon should have all possible tests now, and then he should be sent home. Full stop. No re-call. In view of his fears it would be almost abusive to drag him back to hospital. Holistically, physical care needs to be balanced with his mental and emotional condition. Peace of mind, and being safely with his own people are more important than endless tests... I completely trust your judgment, I will support you in all your decisions, as you weigh up the options and choose to be merciful... This is not 'Do Not Resuscitate'. That's a different issue... As long as Gordon is with us, God has a purpose for him. Maybe we won't ever see the full picture, but – what a picture! The family's praying for you all...

Abigail, our daughter, suggested that the depression medication probably caused Gordon's acute constipation. By the following day, Saturday, he was in better form, enjoying the Changing of the Guard as his staff members came and went. He was even willing for them to take time out to visit the loo. Lynn, our volunteer Geraldine, all his carers took a turn. Antibiotics were prescribed. Aspirin and beta blockers became part of his life. His coffee habit may have been a factor in his heart condition, so decaff was specified.

I emailed an update to our daughters and son.

> This level of illness may be a first for Peacehaven... staff members' duty hours have been extended, and volunteers and part-time carers have joined the team... such grace, such an outpouring of love into Gogo's life.

Isabel Nolan, our friend, said that if he ever has to go into hospital again she will go to be with him and do the night shifts. I could ask for no better friend for him.

Denise was on bedside duty on Sunday, and found Gordon in much better form. She brought her laptop and they watched some films and played cards.

> He's beyond keen to get home but he is so much more at peace, and is eating and drinking. I've emailed you a little picture!

I forwarded it to the family. Susie responded 'I love that shot, what a sweet little man.' He was so relaxed that on Monday evening he was happy to tell Lynn to go home before he went asleep. He had had some visitors, including the pastor of the church, one of his chums. When Gordon was at home in Peacehaven, the pastor, Erich Fischer, regularly visited him and read the Bible with him and they prayed together.

The next day Gordon went home and settled down, but there were times when the deep anxiety haunted him. On 1st February he bravely went out for a ten-minute drive with Geraldine, whom he loves to bits.

Whatever about having heart disease, Gordon's eyesight was deteriorating and his hearing didn't seem good. Nor was his mental health robust.

When Gogo had started to stay at home, and showed such fear at going out, we had at first wondered if something horrible had happened to him in town. After careful open questioning, Salome concluded that Gordon had suffered a heart incident when he was out, and that he had probably been feeling the physical effects for some time, profound tiredness and weakness, heaviness and possibly pain. He couldn't understand what was happening to him, and couldn't explain anything to anybody.

A 'heart attack' can bring with it a catastrophic sense of doom – a threat to life, not from acquired knowledge, but from an instinctive sense that one is under attack. Gordon's anxiety, his panic at the idea of ever having to go out again, seems eminently rational.

20

THE COMFORTERS

I may assert Eternal Providence,
And justify the ways of God to men.

Milton, Paradise Lost

IN mid January Denise sent a memo to the staff, detailing the increased support that Gordon needed during the day and the night. This covered everything from bedroom cleaning to retirement activities to give him some interests. In every area of care, the emphasis was on giving him choices, inviting him to take steps, enabling him to do things. There was a new Diary provided to record his eating and liquid intake; there was another Diary in which to record his behavioural responses to being ill or troubled – such as retching, urinating in the wrong place, panic attacks, extreme anxiety.

The relationship of staff members with Gordon was to respect his wishes and his need for privacy, as well as assuring him of support, without pressure. 'Gordon, is it ok if I go into your room to get your clothes? I'm going to put your clothes in the washing machine, would you like to help me? We can do it together if you like.'

> If cleaning his room, try to encourage him to keep you company, and he can play music while you work. He does not necessarily need to do anything, but he may surprise you.

The morning routine included gentle chatting while waking him up, putting on his music, asking him what he would like to wear today, taking him through bathing with help where he might need it, giving him privacy to use the toilet first, and to dry himself after his bath. If Gordon became anxious or started to retch due to stress, the staff member would withdraw and the anxiety usually subsided after a few moments.

Bedtime was given its own protective and comforting routine. One evening Gordon had been found sitting half naked and retching due to anxiety, so, after he said goodnight staff were asked to make sure he was 'safe in bed and cosy'. There would be soft lighting all night with a system of lamps and nightlights, in his room and the hall and the landing. Some staff members found that praying with him at bedtime seemed to calm him.

In these days of retirement Gordon would enjoy visitors, and a staff member could sit with him and play a game or do crafts, or kick a football around. He might enjoy that. Be creative, but do ask him.

Denise prepared a statement on Gordon's Medical Needs and possible steps to be taken in the future. Gordon's re-entry into Peacehaven has been difficult. Doctors came at intervals to monitor his heart rate and take bloods, and to prescribe for his anxiety. Denise asked the psychiatrist to come to visit Gordon as the current medication wouldn't be a long-term solution, and the staff team might need more support. Gordon's sight was deteriorating, he was displaying possible heart disease, and his mental health had deteriorated over the last year. The doctor discussed the possibility that Gordon might need to be admitted to a nursing home if he required medical care.

The people looking after Gordon would work as a team. This would include staff and GP and psychiatric advisors, with all reports and updates being sent to the GP. He was also given copies of Denise's instructions to the staff and details of all Gordon's medication.

This experience of illness in the house was new. Gordon was starving himself and he didn't drink enough, even when encouraged. He needed to stay hydrated, as this directly affected his heart rate and blood pressure.

My family and close friends were due an update. I wrote,

> This afternoon I visited Peacehaven to meet Lily and Denise, Gordon's keyworker. Denise has designed detailed measures to support him in all aspects of his day, and the staff are putting them into practice.

Some of the coaxing approaches rang an irreverent bell with me from many years ago. I remember my second small daughter refusing to get into the buggy, and her manipulative mother asking sweetly 'Do you want me to lift you in, or can you climb in all by yourself?' And the little one climbing in like a (deluded) lamb.

I continued,

> Almost every breath Gogo takes is monitored and noted down, every crumb he eats, every panic-driven action. He is loved. While we were talking together both Lily and Denise got glitters in their eyes and I had a tiny weep. Denise said all the staff have their moments of sorrow for the little guy who used to rule the roost. They're offering him chocolate to tempt him to eat. Lynn made luscious chocolate buns. All the doctors have all his notes. They're like a fan club.
>
> You may pray, but don't worry. When Gogo's usefulness on earth is done, he'll be whisked away, and for all eternity he'll never stop talking!

There were at least six appointments in place during the following month, and Gordon would not be willing to attend them. If he were to be enabled to go, two staff members would have to take him. It seemed that extra staff would be needed.

History gets thicker as it approaches recent times.

A.J.P.Taylor, Historian

It is getting thicker. Gordon's story is coming closer to Now, and I'm focusing on details. There are no more broad sweeps, skimming over months and years at a time. Events are jostling each other.

On 13th February 2012 Gordon became very unwell, and I got a text from staff member Sally telling me that he was back in hospital for a check-up and tests.

After Gordon spent that night in A&E, Peacehaven quickly made the decision to take him home, and to have him treated privately. Unless he was actually dying, as a public patient he might have had to wait a long time for the HSE to sort him out. Money wasn't a problem. He could pay for treatment. His Disability Allowance is carefully managed for him by Peacehaven, and since he hasn't been in the habit of spending much, there was enough for this unforeseen emergency.

Denise and Salome, all the staff, were talking Gordon through these events, quietly and peacefully, explaining and simplifying, and his anxiety levels were low, no panicking. They spoke about nursing home as a future possibility. An application was made to have his name put on the waiting list of a nursing home in Greystones, should the time come when, through refusing food and drink, he would need nursing beyond the skill of the Peacehaven staff.

Two days later he was in St Vincent's University Hospital having a heart scan. Lily emailed me, and the Board,

> Just to let you know that Gordon arrived back at Peacehaven yesterday afternoon. He was in good form, with hugs for everyone! Salome and Sally took him to hospital this morning for tests, he was in good spirits

> and went without too much fuss. Great to see him home and happy!

I wrote to Geoffrey, fellow Board member for many years.

> I'm touched beyond words (but not quite!) at the loving creative energy the staff are wrapping round Gordon. I can't imagine any single aspect of his care which could be improved upon.

Alan Egar, my cousin living in Yorkshire, can't drop in for coffee with Gordon, but he phones him for a chat. Now and then he has sent him a railway magazine, the perfect gift. He told me that recently he got a good response, and there was a great feeling of closeness together. He prayed with Gogo, while they were on the phone.

We rejoiced that he had eaten some dinner. In early February Gordon was doing well, going out for short drives with Denise and with Geraldine. There was an appointment for 29th February for Gordon to see the cardiac consultant, to discuss the results of the echo scan which was done weeks previously. He had been a little bit gloomy for a few days. We prayed that he would stride into the consultant's room and reach out his hand for a good shake. Cousin Alan phoned Peacehaven to speak to Gordon and 'jolly him along', and again he prayed with him. And Salome made enquiries, and decided that she would go alone to consult the consultant, and *Gordon didn't need to go.*

In Galway, Maggie Murray was living a Gordon-free life, which made her sad. As she prepared for her retirement party Margaret wrote to me, saying that her chosen field of work, among people with intellectual disabilities, was all Gordon's fault.

> He is in my thoughts often, but especially as I come to the end of my chapter working in intellectual disability

> – for now. He joined me so often in my office, sorting out the bundles of paper and files, visiting with me on home visits and partaking at team meetings. And only Gordon could get away with letting us know when it was time to wrap up – he was bored. Give him my love.

I hadn't known any of this! When Gordon was visiting in Galway, Margaret couldn't stop all her work to entertain him. So she spoke to her team manager and the team members, and there was no problem with Margaret being shadowed by this most charming gentleman, who was himself symbolic of her work. When a house visit needed to be made, Margaret phoned in advance, asking the family if Gordon could come, saying that he would happily sit in another room reading his newspaper.

> In his wisdom he always knew when it was time to go home and would come in to us, paper under his arm and call me to task. Or else, perhaps, happily join us for a cup of tea.
>
> And of course he wouldn't ever breathe a word of what was discussed, or what information was contained in the various papers he tidied!

... and everything was in its Proper Place.

Hans Andersen

Much earlier in this story I wrote,

> If Gordon's life is a tapestry, it's stitched together by trains.

This stage of his life was different. There were no train journeys now to thread orderly lines through his days. Life was perplexing, full of new situations and predicaments and difficult decisions.

Thinking about it, I see instead an unfinished jigsaw puzzle and a topsy-turvy pile of pieces. As each piece is put into place, the picture is more clear. The best of all jigsaws are the special wooden ones that include whimsies, little pieces that are cut into precise shapes that complement the theme of the picture. These Wentworth puzzles are much loved in my family. I've paid tribute to Gordon by choosing the best jigsaws in the world to help me to tell his story.

In this Gordon Jigsaw the little whimsies would be cut in the shapes of trains, aeroplanes, buses, Christmas trees, briefcases, ham sandwiches, umbrellas, ties, cufflinks. Could a whimsy be cut in the shape of a pair of socks? Could Wentworth make a Springer Spaniel? Gordon has loved all our dogs, except for the one bitter episode when Springer stole his shirt.

It's time to watch a jigsaw piece being put in place. It's in the shape of a bed, heaped with duvet and rugs. My brother's bedroom had become an increasingly important part of his life.

The third Peacehaven house, in Applewood Heights, also in Greystones, had been radically altered and fitted out to provide more independent accommodation for four residents. Several of the men and women had spent trial periods there, and in due course four people went to live in Applewood.

One of these gentlemen had lived in the Peacehaven House along with Gordon. Being physically disabled and unable to manage the stairs, he had occupied the downstairs bedroom, until his move to Applewood some time ago, where he settled in quickly, leaving his former bedroom empty. He was happy and contented in his new home.

My brother's heart may have been doing its very best for him, but the doctor wasn't taking any chances. Gordon was not to climb stairs again. He must have a bedroom on the ground floor. In mid-March Gordon's personal stuff was installed in the recently vacated downstairs room and he took possession not only of his new ground-floor bedroom, but also of his own en suite bathroom. He had every comfort, and if he got tired of company he could slip away to his room to be quiet. A piece shaped like a comfy bed was tapped into place in the jigsaw.

A whimsy in the shape of a pair of spectacles might be too difficult for the cutters to make, but it would be very relevant to my brother's life. Gordon and glasses have always had an uneasy relationship. Some time before he moved to the ground floor, when he was on his way downstairs, he tripped and toppled over, down the last few steps. He cut his eyebrow, which would mend. But he also broke his glasses, smashed them. Without them he was almost blind. No problem – a new pair of glasses which had been ordered *weeks previously* arrived in perfect time. You could consider that an amazing coincidence, or God's provision. Another, specially cut, whimsy was clicked into place to celebrate the new glasses.

Though in general, and in principle from his own point of view, Gordon was not going out, in fact he did have occasional little adventures. He went for a short car ride to Fred and Ruth's house for coffee. He's known Salome's parents all his life, and Fred has known Gogo's parents since he himself was a boy. Gordon is becoming comfortable with short trips, he's under no pressure and his mood is mostly happy. Denise and Salome talk him through everything. He trusts them.

Why don't we get a coffee-mug whimsy? Everybody who calls to see Gordon is offered coffee, and when he gets a burst of courage and goes to visit someone, coffee is produced. A coffee-mug whimsy is slipped gently into its unique spot.

21

WHAT NEXT?

SOME day Gordon will die. So Salome discussed his funeral with him, and they made plans. Why would they not do this? Somebody needed to. As they chatted, with no pressure, Gordon made his wishes clear. He knows that he won't be present. Over years it's been explained to him that he'll go to be with Jesus (and with mum and dad for good measure!) and then he'll be strong and well, and he'll never be tired or frightened.

The funeral service will be in Hillside Church in Greystones, where his mother's funeral took place. More recently Gordon has attended the Nazarene Community Church, where he's had lovely times, 'meeting and greeting' at the door, singing duets with Fred – and shaking countless grateful hands. But Hillside Church is his historic place, where he went with his parents during the early years in Greystones, and to which he has chosen to return.

Gordon would like Fred to lead the service. Who else would he choose?

Seán and I will deliver eulogies. Eulogies? About Gordon! What will we say? Seán, a wise and experienced staff member, is a great friend. He's been on all sorts of big and small trips with Gordon. I want to hear his eulogy! Me – either I'll choke up and have to retire in confusion, or they'll pull my coat tails to make me stop talking and sit down.

There will be singing. Gordon has chosen the hymns,

1. To God be the Glory, Great things He has done.

2. Great is Thy Faithfulness, O God my Father, There is no shadow of turning with Thee.

3. O Lord my God, when I in awesome wonder consider all the works Thy hand has made, I see the stars...

For the final hymn he chose,

4. God sent His Son, they called Him Jesus. He came to love, heal and forgive... Because He lives, I can face tomorrow.

Salome will play the piano, beautifully.

Gordon chose that his body would be buried in Redford, with his parents' bodies. I did some telephoning to ascertain whether this could be done, and I was readily given all the detailed information I needed.

Arrangements are in place.

This is not a mournful or gloomy part of the story, although when Gordon's funeral eventually takes place, tears will surely spill. There are still some little shapely gaps in the jigsaw. I'm rummaging in my whimsy bag. Out pops the shape of a big book, and on the picture side in curly writing is *Messiah!* It's the score for his beloved Messiah, and it fits into its space. My fingers poke around, and a round-shaped piece comes out. It's a cabbage? Of course not! It's the big green hydrangea blossom which used to sprout from Gordon's button-hole. That piece looks beautiful in the jigsaw. And remember the splendour of his shoes? Into the bag go my questing fingers, and they bring out a whimsy shaped like a pair of shoes, gleaming black, *and with the laces tied in big bows.*

From all this serious stuff, I must briefly turn to shoe-laces. The little, young Gordon-boy eventually learned to tie his shoe-laces, and as with so many of his hard-won skills, having learned it, he couldn't stop doing it. It began to seem that every time he sat down, he untied his laces, yanked them tighter, and tied them again. Tighter. His feet almost developed waistlines. Under that abuse, the laces broke. He tied the bits together. That doesn't work, knots are the worst thing in a shoelace. So he went hunting for replacements. Dad wore shoes with laces, so there might be a spare pair Gordon could pinch. Otherwise, he did the obvious thing – needs must – and took the laces out of dad's second pair of shoes.

My father only wore one kind of shoe, shiny black with a toecap, known as an Oxford. Very conservative shoes, they were so much part of his everyday outfit that one young friend used to assume that Christian men only wore black Oxfords. Dad was good with laces, adjusting the bow symmetrically, always tidy. Gordon, emulating his dad, was committed to black shoes with laces.

After he came to live with us, he would steal his brother-in-law's shoe-laces! Unfortunately they were brown, but with maturity Gordon was accepting compromise. Eventually I fed his obsession by buying industrial quantities of them, black ones, just for Gordon.

Since moving to live in Peacehaven, Gordon's feet have had a complete makeover. They don't know themselves – or each other. They're clad in slip-ons, trainers, shoes with Velcro fastenings. Those changes began to be made just as the number of socks on each foot was being reduced, and since then both feet have been walking on air.

I must fish the last few whimsies out of the bag. A bus time-table would be fun, an easy shape to cut, and it would slot into its place. Gordon loved sharing special friendships in church, and taking communion, so another whimsy would show a wineglass with a little piece of bread beside it. Oh – a big trans-atlantic aeroplane whimsy would be essential, and another one would be shaped like a wheelie suitcase.

The final whimsy to be fitted into its space could be a cross, not a crucifix, an empty cross, because Jesus, risen, would be triumphantly waiting in heaven for Gordon to arrive. I can't say what will happen, the best I can imagine would be inadequate. But – God sees Gordon coming, and goes to welcome him, saying, 'Well done, good and faithful Gordon. Come and share my joy!'

Gordon understands perfectly, his face is radiant, he goes forward to meet the Lord, and *they shake hands.*

Where there's a Will...

People get gloomy about making wills, and then they try to have a discussion, and that may become contentious, and then it's all too difficult, so it's put off for another day. Then somebody dies intestate, and the trouble really starts. Or so I'm told. I know some families have had interesting episodes concerning wills, as elderly relations die.

As a family we've missed out on the quarrels. The disposal of assets has been benevolently achieved. Not without some interesting incidents, as on the day when I walked through Dublin from one bank to another, with what seemed to me to be a vast number of banknotes in my bag. I felt as though I was in a thriller, and everybody watching the film knew that something terrible was certain to happen. Nothing happened. I got away with it.

The staff members who supported Gordon's life knew what the next step should be after drawing up funeral plans, and they conferred with me about it.

It was time for Gordon to make a will.

I took the first step on the 13th June by phoning our solicitor, who had been so supportive when my dad was ill. He had decided to take time out to study, and had passed his practice over to someone else. I phoned the 'someone else', to discuss Gordon's need to make a will, and our suggestion that, bearing Gordon's disability in mind and the circumstances under which he lived, the solicitor might like to do the work pro bono. He was charming, and we had a good conversation. He would discuss the matter and report back to me very shortly. He suggested that he and a colleague might visit my brother in Peacehaven. Super. He asked me quite a bit about Gordon's level of understanding. I felt that there was an attitude of personal and flexible service.

I followed up the conversation with an appreciative, detailed, email, to encourage him.

On 2nd July Denise told me that a new solicitor had been recommended to her, by the second one I had spoken to. She emailed him. When he didn't respond we were philosophic. Solicitors took their time; they were desperately busy, and it would be bad form for us to fuss.

When I came home from holidays on the 24th July, I visited Peacehaven to take part in the Annual Meeting which Peacehaven has with each resident, their family, their keyworker, the house manager, and the company manager. That was Gordon, me, Denise, Salome and Lily. We sat in one of the living rooms – with hindsight it might have impressed Gordon better if we had gathered round a conference table. He wasn't much impressed, even though it was all about him. He was the reason for the meeting. While the rest of us felt very businesslike as Denise took us through the items for discussion, Gordon did what Gordon does. He sat in his armchair, legs well apart, resting his elbows on his knees, picking absent-mindedly at his fingers, musing, remote from the topics under discussion. Now and then Denise would call his attention, to answer a question or to give his point of view. We were busy respecting Gordon. He didn't give a fig for our cogitations, all about him. He daydreamed.

It was a general update, and since Gordon's Will still didn't exist, we had very little to say about it. I was given material to study from Inclusion Ireland, relating to managing a Patient's Private Property (PPP) Account, and advised about the National Parents and Siblings Alliance, npsa.ie.

It could be truthfully said that Gogo wouldn't care if decisions were made behind his back, made for him instead of with him.

I made suggestions about The Will, and I emailed them to Lily. Everything, if not in triplicate, was at least very carefully documented.

Lazily, time passed. It was high summer. No hurry about anything. Solicitors are entitled to take holidays. We didn't have any sense of urgency about Gordon's still non-existent will, though an *existent* will would have pleased us. Still, courteous as ever, we still didn't fuss.

Then – we had action. In late August a solicitor contacted Denise to talk about the Will. She said to Denise that before making a will, Gordon needed to be seen by a doctor, to determine whether he had the mental capacity to understand the proposed discussion. The doctor visited Gordon, and I have no idea what they talked about. But it was satisfactory, and the doctor certified Gordon as being capable.

The solicitor had been very strict that Gordon must not be coerced or persuaded into making any decisions.

In fact Gogo was very clear about where his money and possessions should go. The solicitor went away to write up the will, which she emailed to Denise. Denise in turn read it to Gordon for his approval. A partner in the solicitor's firm came to sign it with Gordon and a witness.

Gordon used to love visiting his bank to lodge and withdraw money, but he had lost his former interest in business. It was no doubt because he had retired, and he shouldn't have to attend to business any more. He was happy for his bank account to be managed by Peacehaven, so Denise and Salome have signed up to take care of that on his behalf.

We have on our hands a sick man, – a seriously sick man.

Nicholas I, Emperor of Russia, attributed

12th May 2012. Another day, another hospital – this time to St Michael's in Dun Laoghaire, for an echo cardio scan. Gordon was given a warm welcome, some of the staff members recognising him from the train. That was a happy bonus, for everybody.

It was agreed that, when possible, home visits would be made, to avoid frightening hospital appointments. Gordon's heart was abnormally enlarged, with low blood pressure, and an irregular beat. It was leaking. I was told that it was performing at less than fifty per cent – of what? How is that measured? Anyway, it sounded pretty serious.

Denise told me that Peacehaven were determined to keep Gordon at home, rather than move him to the nursing home, which could break his heart. An apt metaphor.

Later in May Denise and Peter visited the Heart Failure Clinic (Education Class) in St Michael's. They went on Gordon's behalf. They came away with six pages of advice, new information and instructions. Peter wrote,

> Denise and I attended...on Gordon's behalf as we were advised by the clinic it would be better for staff to attend, and there was no need to put Gordon through the anxiety of an unnecessary extra trip to hospital to sit through an hour-long class that staff could attend, in his place.

The material was detailed, covering every possible aspect of Gordon's life, from the daily significance of his weight, through advice on appetite, exercise, symptoms to watch out for, breathlessness and diet, to how to manage travelling! Ironic that, for a man who could hardly bear to leave the house. A formidable list of medications included an analysis of the purpose of each one.

Denise and Peter could phone the clinic to discuss concerns at any time. The hospital staff were friendly and helpful, and Peter told me that Gordon won them over – as he always does. People do seem to warm to him, and love him.

He had to go to hospital again in June, and he was very distressed. His heart rate was critically high, and the beta blocker dose was increased. Afterwards, the local doctor came to check how he was. The Heart Clinic planned that a nurse would visit Gordon, to spare him the hospital nightmare. Apart from that, Denise told me he was in great form.

And he was! The new medication was effective, and Gordon was doing wonderfully well. The community nurse visited him monthly.

He rose early and showered with minimal support. He made

his own breakfast and sandwiches and coffee. Staff began to involve him in morning activities, to interest him, such as reading the newspaper, experimenting with arts and crafts, going for a drive, or doing chores. I suspect there may have been a bit of muttering when chores were suggested. 'After all I've been through, you expect me to do housework?' But Denise had her priorities right, and Gordon was being gently encouraged to take responsibility for some of his laundry, helping with ironing and doing dishwasher work. Unsurprisingly, he didn't embrace his renewed responsibilities. When a trip in the car was suggested, he usually chose not to leave the house.

22

HOW DO I LOVE THEE?

For ever wilt thou love, and she be fair!

John Keats, Ode on a Grecian Urn

IN August a Wedding was announced! Gordon's most favourite social occasion. A gowned bride, beautifully dressed guests, women in high heels. And he was invited. On the day his best clothes were laid out, a flower was chosen to dress his buttonhole, and a driver was engaged to take him, and possibly some other guests as well. Gogo didn't have a monopoly of privilege.

But it all went wrong. Getting ready was worrying for him, he couldn't make his breakfast go down, he felt doomed going out to the car, and arriving at the church was dreadful. The friend who drove him there went into the church with him, but terror was boiling up, and he panicked and began to retch. He had done his very best, and he was brought home to safety.

On another day, in Tesco with Denise, the involuntary expression of fear took over again, and he began to retch.

The specialist nurse prescribed stronger diuretic medication, a long-term remedy to relieve stress on his heart.

In September Keith and I flew away to Malta for two weeks. We had discussed the possibility of a Gordon-crisis. Firstly, we trusted the Peacehaven staff to make wise decisions, and secondly, in an emergency we would get home with all speed. There was no crisis. We came home as planned.

Autumn met us in its abundant beauty. We began to look ahead to Christmas.

Since Gordon was born in 1953 I had never spent a Christmas without him, either in Clontarf or in Rathfarnham. Now, in 2012 we were looking ahead to Christmas, and Gordon was rooted so deeply in Greystones that, even if he could be persuaded to come away, wrenched away, his roots would be left behind. His wellspring was in Peacehaven. He couldn't leave. Customarily Peacehaven closed for a couple of days over Christmas. What would we do? What could we do? Our children and grandchildren, twelve people, were knitted into our Christmas Day in Rathfarnham.

Denise decided to stay with Gordon in Peacehaven over Christmas.

Not only Denise. We were still helplessly stuttering 'Thank you! Oh thank you!' when we were told that Wilf and Michelle, Denise's parents, were coming to spend Christmas with Denise and Gordon. I visited Peacehaven on Christmas Eve, and Gordon was completely happy, safe in his own home, with three people whom he loved.

November had been a momentous month, because while arrangements for Gordon's Christmas were being put in place, another future event was being planned.

I chose my wife, as she her wedding gown, not for a fine glossy surface, but such qualities as would wear well.

Oliver Goldsmith, The Vicar of Wakefield

'Bum, bum, ba-bum, bum bum ba-bum.' That, as you may not have guessed, is Here Comes the Bride, the simplified version, vocalised by Gordon. You might prefer to listen to Wagner's original composition, in Lohengrin. It's a question of taste, really.

The outburst of Here Comes the Bride was because in November Salome and her beloved, Niall, announced their engagement! It was a red-letter month for them, and it was a rosy-faced time for Gordon. He was incandescent! Radiant! Over the moon! Enchanted! He loved Salome, Niall was a good friend, and he loved weddings. The conjunction was almost unbearable.

However, every silver lining has a cloud, and Peacehaven was under a unique cloud for the next five months. Hardly an hour passed during those many weeks when Gordon didn't point dramatically at his ring finger and sing Here comes the Bride (simplified version), explaining that it was all about 'Omey 'Omey! He sang and pointed, he pointed and sang. The people in his house learned new lessons, to an Advanced Level, of patience and tolerance. They longed for relief, for the Wedding Day on the fourth of April to come. They hoped that afterwards Gogo might pull back on his celebrations.

All Gordon's joyful fantasies were coming together. Salome would wear an exquisite gown, with high heels. There would be dozens, hundreds (literally) of Gordon's friends. Men would be in sharply tailored suits and rich ties. Every buttonhole would carry a flower. The event would be hooge. For Christmas we gave him wedding garments, a silk tie, a perfect shirt, and later Peacehaven bought him a wedding suit. The flower would be organised in good time. Gordon would be the perfect wedding guest.

Was all this just a fantasy on Gordon's part? Was there even a remote hope that he would go to Salome's wedding? It was about eighteen months since he had voluntarily stepped outside the house. The exceptions had been tiny car drives with a staff member. Apart from going out through the front door – unmanageably difficult at times – he was so ill-at-ease in crowds that even at home in Peacehaven, when there were guests for dinner, he sat near the door of the dining room, and escaped when it all got too much. As the day of the wedding came close, Gordon was being gently eased towards the challenge of going. If he could have expressed his intentions, they would have been for him to have a central place in the ceremony, and at the reception and at the party. He said over and over, confidently, that he would be there.

To me it seemed highly unlikely that his courage would override his anxiety. On the Day, with the other wedding guests who were seated in the church waiting for the bride, I was trying unobtrusively to keep an eye on the door, just on the chance that my brother might appear.

He came! Gordon was at Salome's wedding, in his wedding finery, elegantly suited, with a flowery buttonhole, arriving just at the right time with Seán by his side. Unbelievable. We were flooded with joy.

> Human kind cannot bear very much reality.
>
> **T.S.Eliot, Four Quartets**

During Gordon's months of wedding excitement, none of us anticipated the sense of anti-climax he would feel after the long-awaited event was over.

Salome had managed Gordon's devotion perfectly and with a light hand. Clearly, she had explained that though they were good friends, she would never, ever marry him. He understood that.

But he wanted to help, to have a role. Salome would be the star. He could support her on this glorious day. Maybe it wasn't surprising that he offered, as a brotherly gesture, to travel with Salome to the church, in her wedding car. His thinking was clear.

> I thought it would be a friendly thing to do. Wedding cars are huge, there would be lots of room for me and Salome and her dress. We're such good friends. Niall would be pleased to see me keeping Salome company.
>
> She said I couldn't. Fred was going with her. Well, I know he is her dad, but she's grown up! Why does she need her dad in the car?
>
> Then I had another brainwave. I said I would walk up the aisle with Salome. Fred could go and sit with her mum, to keep her company. I would take care of the

Bride, and hold her arm so she wouldn't trip on her beautiful long dress.

They said I couldn't. Fred again.

On the wedding day I was feeling really worried. Seán was with me, he's a very good friend. He somehow helped me to feel better. When he was with me the bad feelings didn't matter so much. I felt really brave. He's a steady sort of man, you feel he could make everything safe.

I have never seen anything like the cars in the car park, and the crowd in the church, hundreds of seats, all full, and everybody chattering and buzzing. The women had gorgeous dresses and crazy hats. They were all waiting for Salome. Seán and I sat at the back near one of the doors, and waited. Ruth (that's my sister, not any of the other Ruths around) came over to give me a huge hug. Her eyes were glittery, and her nose was pink.

Then some little children came in, all dressed in white, with flowers. Then two or three women in long bright silky dresses came in. They all started walking towards the front, so slowly – and Salome came in.

Then, I knew it was OK for Fred to walk with her. He looked so happy!

The Bride, my friend, shimmered with beauty. Her dress was a dream, I knew it would be, but it was her face we saw... she was like the sunshine coming in to meet Niall.

The service was long, lots of singing and speaking – a sermon I suppose. Salome's family sang, starting with just one person singing alone, her cousin Jude. Then more and more, so many of them! Somebody said it was a family flash-mob. That doesn't sound great, but it was magic, it made me want to laugh and

> cry. One of my friends, Jo, who's part of our family, sang a solo. I loved that. I did get very tired, and I felt quite lonely. At the end, when we were outside after the wedding people came down from the front, Salome came and gave me some huge hugs, and now I have photos of it all.
>
> There was a dinner and a party, but I needed to go home. Seán took me and we had some quietness.

Niall and Salome went on honeymoon for three weeks. Gordon's spirits began to sink.

His anxiety and panic attacks erupted, with the familiar distressing symptoms. He'd been through an emotional earthquake, and he couldn't talk about it. I visited him and we sat at the table, I on a kitchen chair and Gordon silent in his comfy padded armchair at the kitchen table, drinking coffee, and we chatted about everything I could think of.

At this stage the staff were concerned, as he wasn't eating enough. They were cooking tasty tempting things, and making soups for him. They were heavy-hearted. Having Gordon sunk in misery was hard for everybody.

I emailed round our family and friends with an update, and I ended,

> Maybe you would pray for – oh, I don't know – a lift of mood, relief from his fear, encouragement for Denise and the other staff treasures who are longing to help him, or – here's an idea! – for the purpose of his life to be fulfilled and for God to take him from this 'vale of tears' to heaven, where he'll never be dumbfounded again.

Isabel responded,

> Gogo is so special, Ruth, he has touched and blessed so

> many people. I'm sure he will continue to do so, until his Heavenly Father comes and takes him to be with Him... He knows what's best for him. Lots and lots of love.

Hilary, my lifelong friend, emailed with prayer for the Lord to work in the best way for Gordon. Maggie Murray was praying for a return of his joie de vivre. Other family members and friends sent messages of love and concern.

Marion, my parents' friend from long ago, emailed,

> Of course I'll pray for dear Gordon and the marvellous staff at Peacehaven... that God's perfect, acceptable and good will, for him and all his loved ones, will be done.

She quoted a little verse that my mother used to sing,

God holds the key of all unknown, and I am glad!
If other hands should hold that key,
or if He trusted it to me,
I might be sad.

Not great poetry. I remember it. It sounds better when it's sung, and my mother sang it, often.

Marion

The FT

TEA IN THE CAB

Eugene's

CHARLIE IN SOUTH HILL

Christmas dinner on 27th September

MICHAEL DOYLE

Home

Erich

WIGGLES THE LABRADOODLE

23

HALLELUJAH!

I BROUGHT a bag of Maltesers with the Daily Express on my next visit. Gordon hugged me – he's such a tender-hearted hugger. If a certain remarkable woman hadn't already been doing it all over the world, I'm sure my specially gifted brother could find he had a vocation for hugging all and sundry, and become celebrated countrywide, if not internationally. There would always be the option of a manly handshake, for those who didn't do hugs.

As I write, in 2013, Gordon is ageing, his hearing isn't good, his eyesight is bad, he has a dysfunctional heart. None of that will improve. He has become happy again. There are many positives. Denise tells me that he's eating well, enjoying the dinner rota in which each resident chooses the meal once a week. Gordon's choice is roast chicken, the everyday version of his birthday and Christmas feasts. His health is steady. His weight is staying at the right level.

He phones for a chat, or I phone him, and we talk nonsense, and he roars with laughter, he has such a sense of fun. The Dublin – Rosslare railway line was closed due to a crash at the Merrion Gates level crossing, and he was enchanted. This was Gordon's commuter line before he retired. He phoned me and we told each other gleefully how many people would be late to work, late home, worried, cross, lose their jobs, miss meeting their friends, be starving hungry, because of the catastrophe. We squeezed every bit of emotion and drama out of it, and Gordon chuckled and chortled.

He goes out for short drives. Peter and he go to the harbour, and, poignantly, to the station, to watch the trains. On the day of the catastrophe they checked for themselves that no trains were coming through. He loves people to drop in for coffee.

Marion Smith, a music therapist, comes every week to make joyful noises with Gordon. He has a super sense of rhythm, and he plays percussion as though born to it, while Marion plays gentle jazz on the keyboard.

A companion dog, Wiggles the labradoodle, visits with his minder regularly. Maybe Gordon would someday find himself going comfortably out through the door for an epic 60-second stroll with Wiggles?

Pastor Erich calls in at the weekend and he and Gordon read the Bible and pray together.

In trying to enrich Gordon's life socially and find interests for him, the staff are letting him lead the way, supporting any notions he might have. They understand him.

There are ups and downs. Gordon sometimes disappears into bed, at other times he'll enjoy a sociable cup of tea. He is content.

Though the Lord is on high, he looks upon the lowly.
The Lord will fulfil his purpose for me.

David, the psalmist

EPILOGUE

THE engine driver yawned. He enjoyed his job, but sometimes it was just too peaceful. Nothing really happens when you're in your cab, rolling along. That's because of all training you get, nothing's meant to happen. It goes like clockwork. For far too long sometimes. He'd really like to get out and go for a walk, the sun was shining.

It was a Bank Holiday Monday, and there were lots of people out and about.

The journey seemed interminable. He'd come from Cork through Mallow and Limerick Junction, which wasn't a town at all, it was in the middle of nowhere. He had trundled through Thurles and Portlaoise, charming places, no doubt, but not to a tired train driver who wanted to get home. Kildare was next and eventually Heuston, Dublin.

He liked Kildare, because next stop would be Dublin, and he liked the long railway embankment running beside the Curragh. He could see in all directions, and on the wide plain he sometimes saw strings of racehorses being exercised.

The racecourse on that day was empty and quiet, but he enjoyed imagining it full of crowds and excitement as people yelled, sometimes in despair, at their favourite, *'Come On!'*

Just past Kildare a few cars had turned off the M7, along the road towards the embankment. One car was parked surprisingly close, and people were relaxing with a picnic. The train left Kildare railway station, picked up speed along the embankment, and began to come closer to the picnickers, and the low rumble grew louder, and you could feel it with your feet.

SKETCH BY CHLOE HANAN

One of the men in the little group leapt up, all a-quiver, galvanised with excitement. He was a short fellow, but somehow he looked ten feet tall. He sped over to the embankment and he stood there, waving his arms, almost levitating, and shouting as the train drew level.

The driver saw him. His hand went to the horn, and he leaned on it. As the sound of the horn tore through the air, out of the engine window stretched an arm and the driver waved, and waved, and his train sped on.

Settled back in his seat, the driver was smiling.

'That' he said to himself, 'was Gordon'.